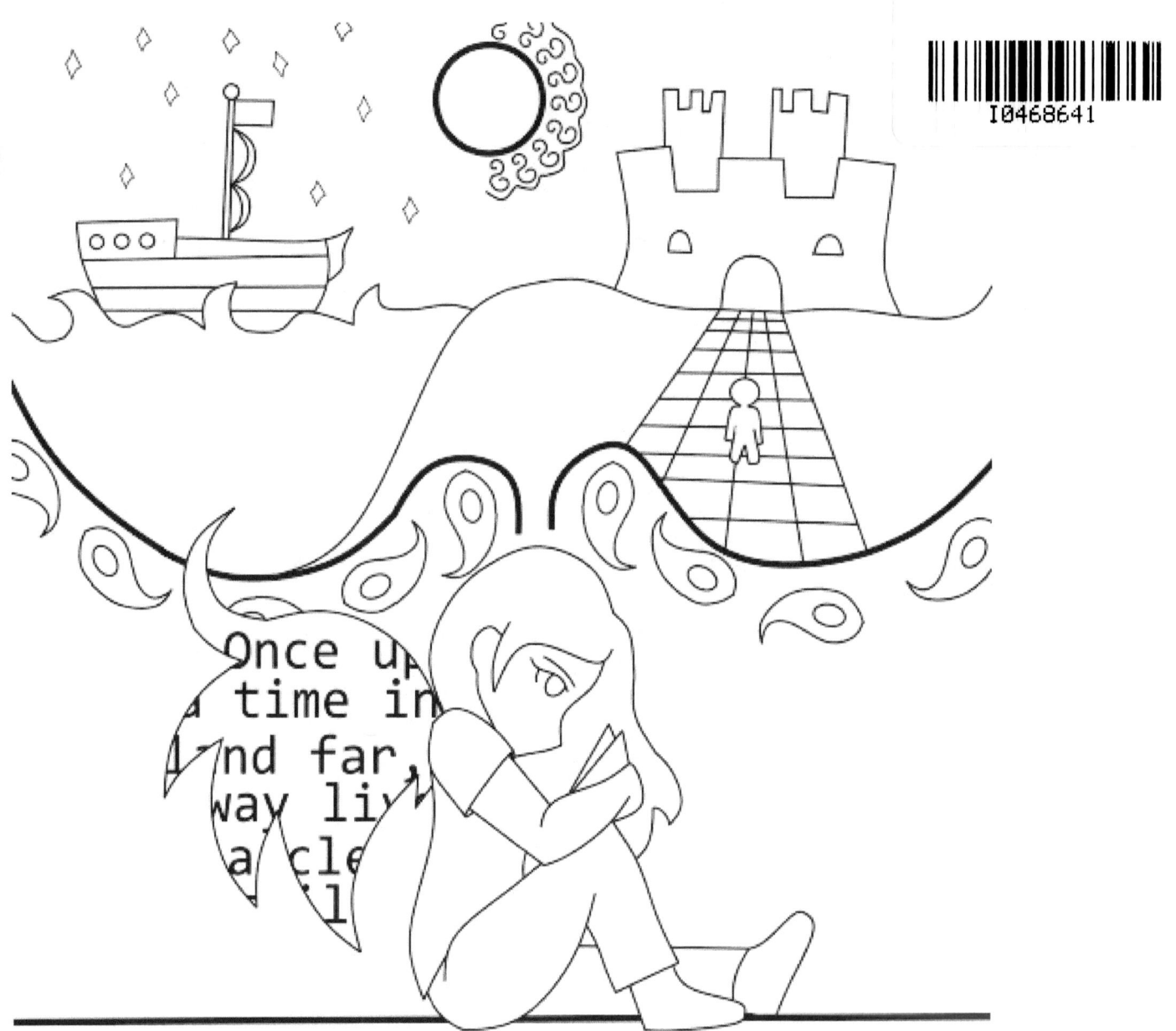

Once up
a time in
nd far,
way li
a cle

I would like to thank those who inspired,

and encouraged me on this adventure.

MP 2016

I0468641

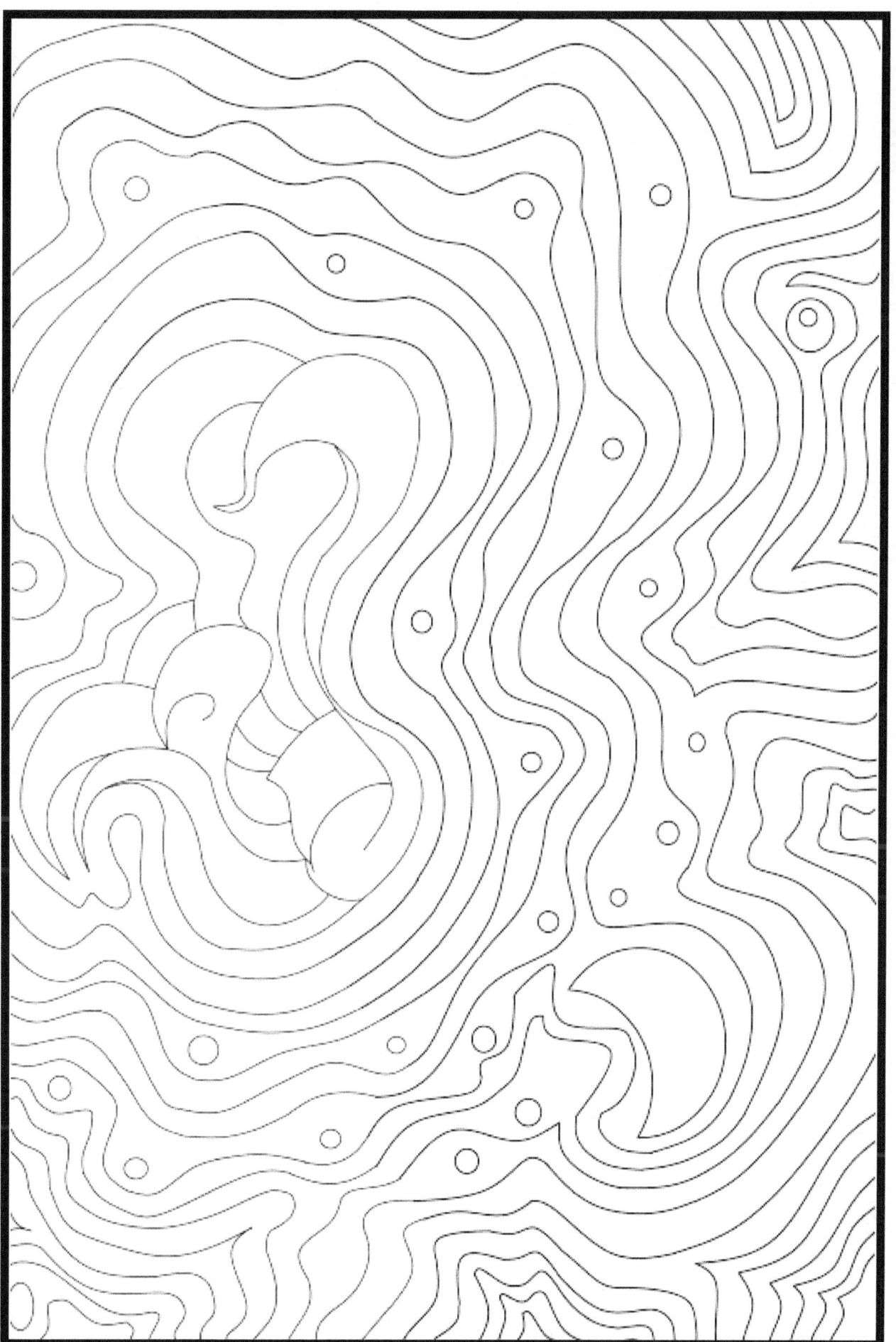

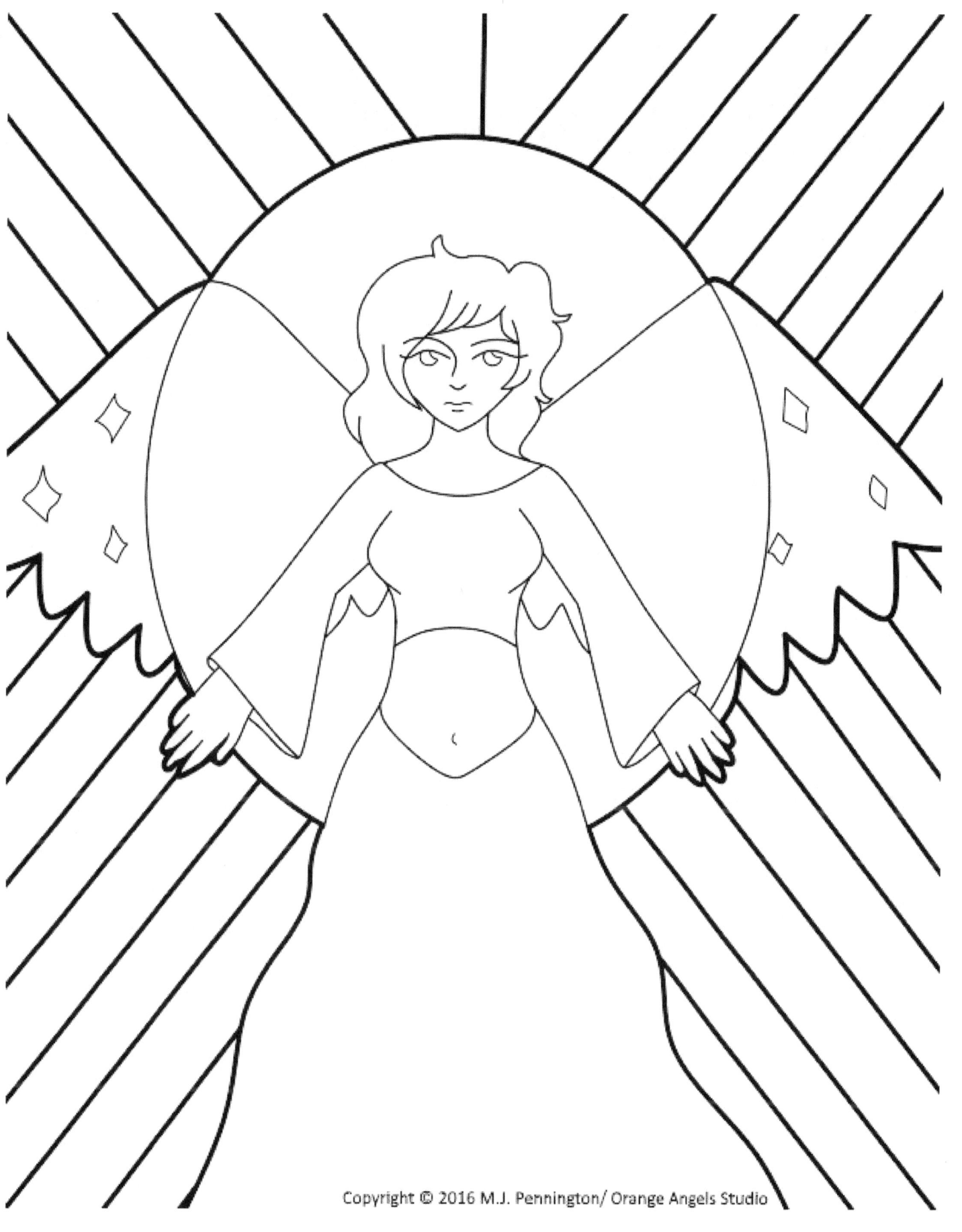

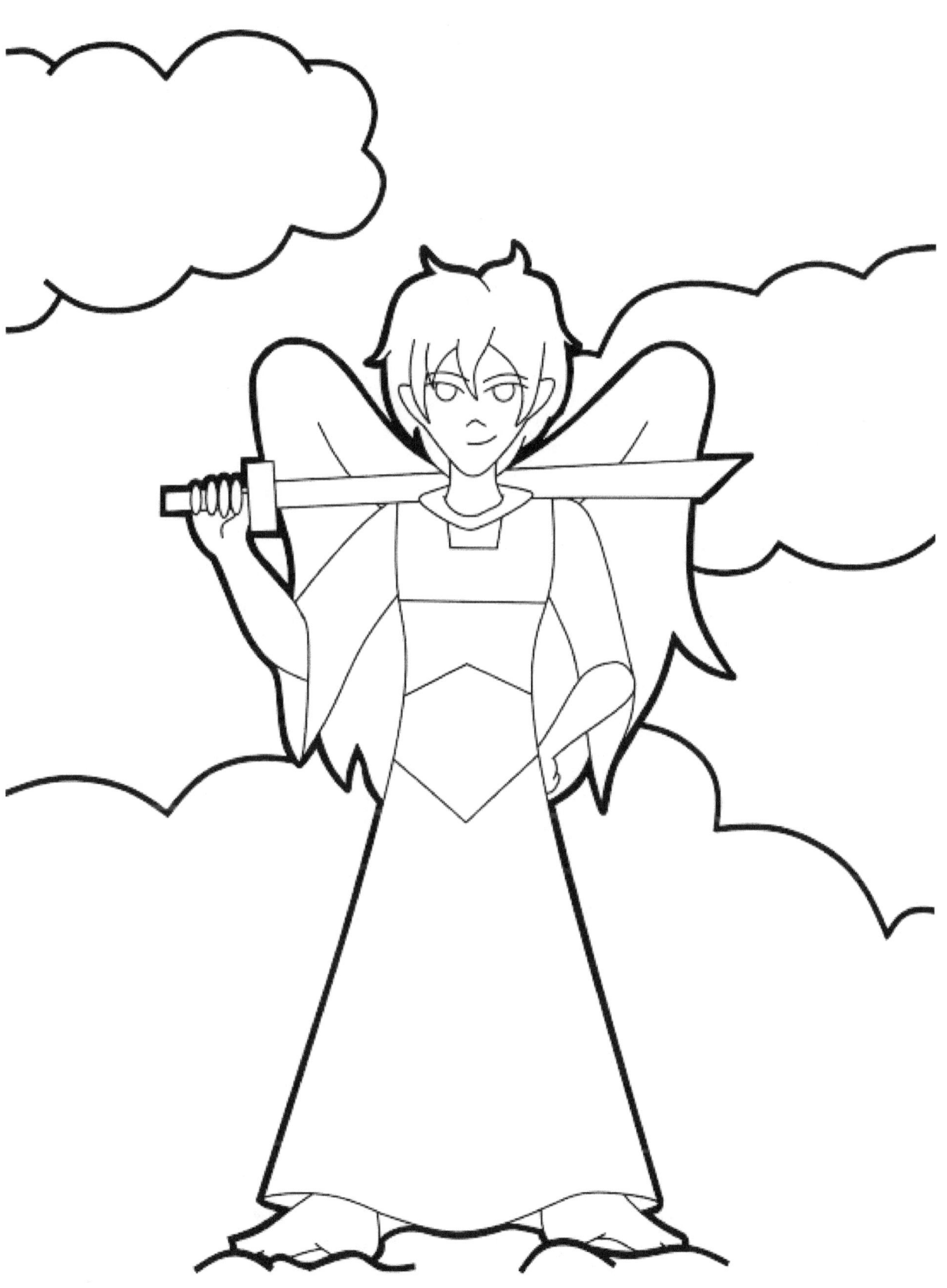

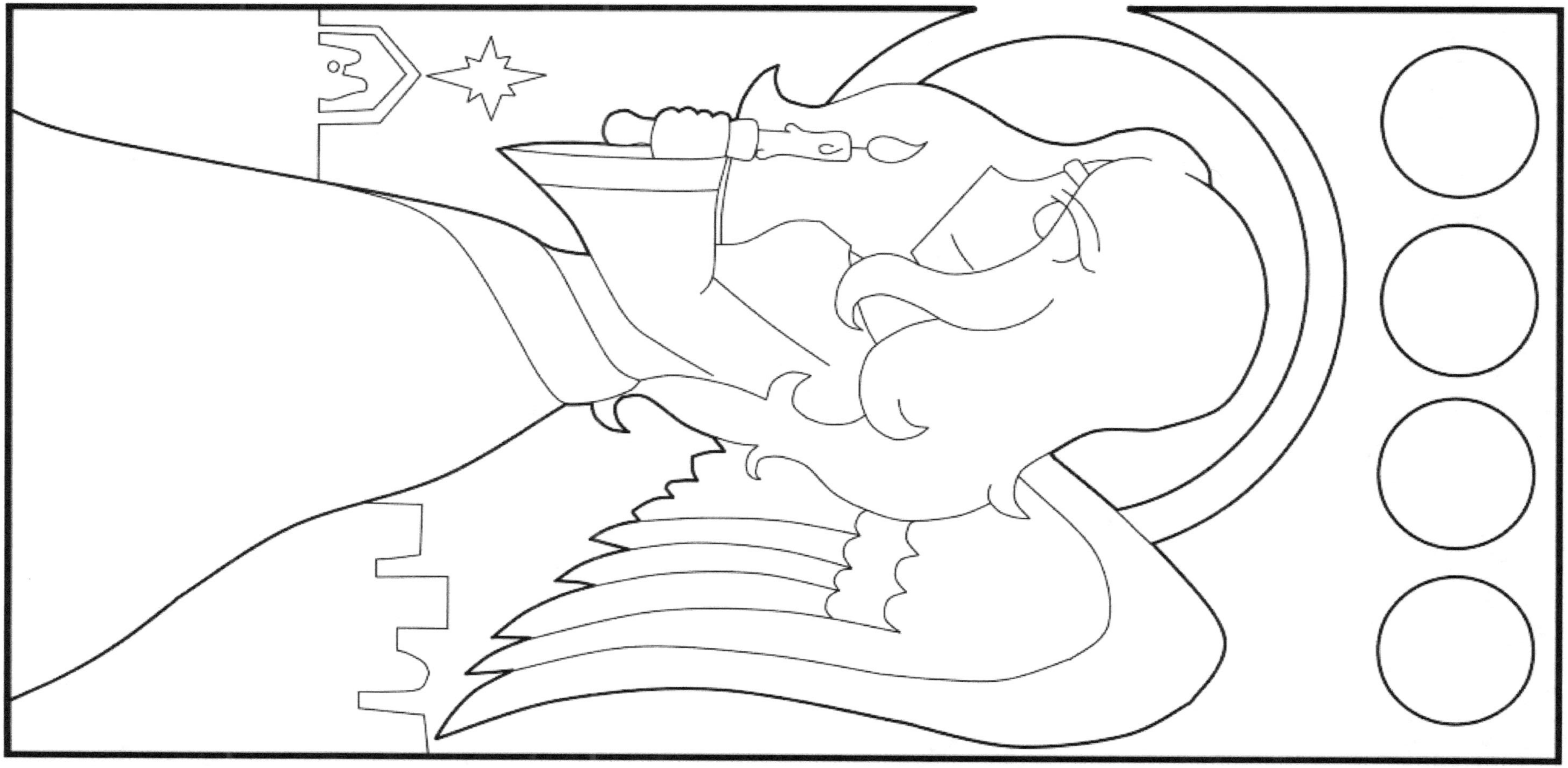

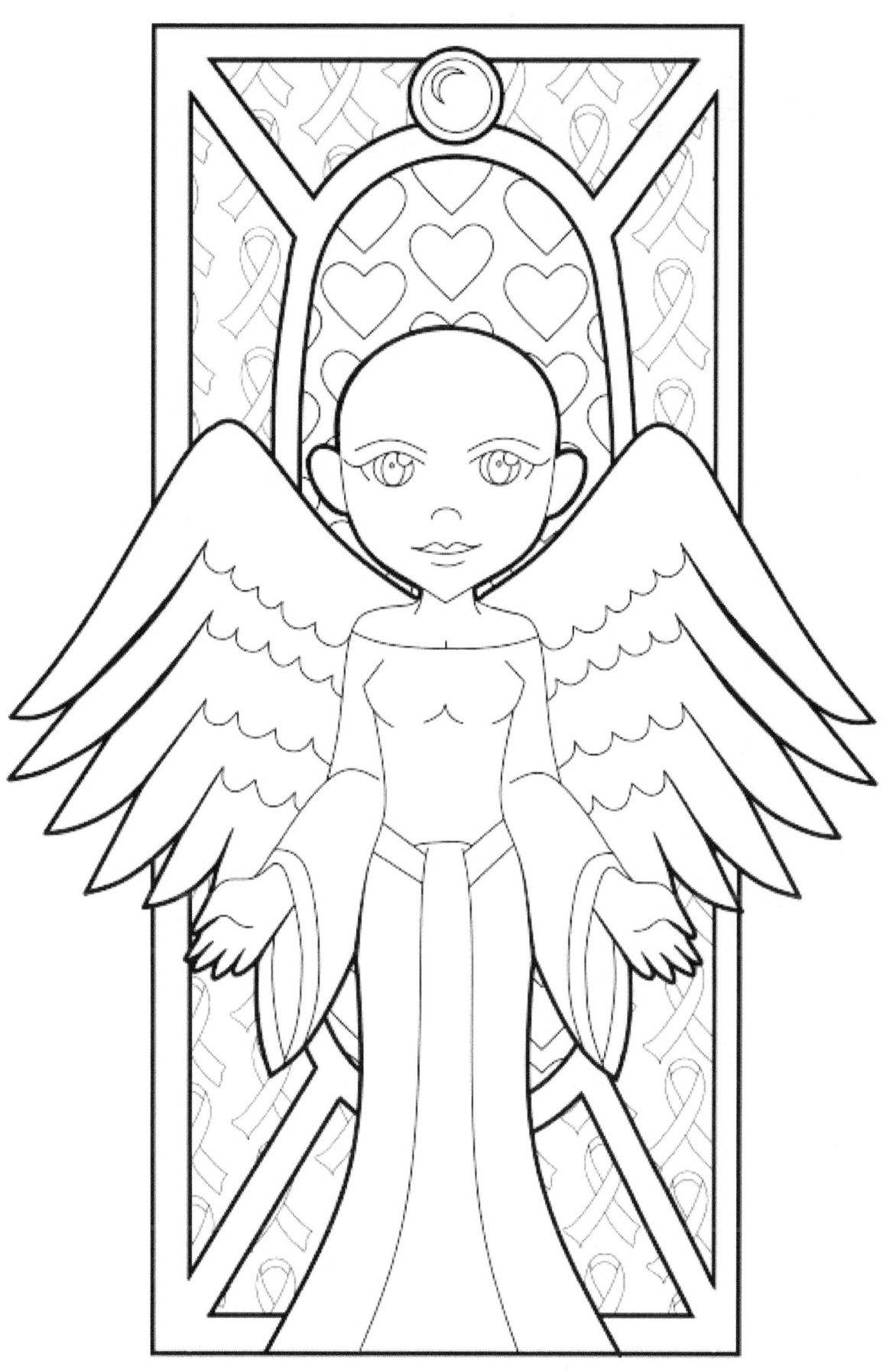

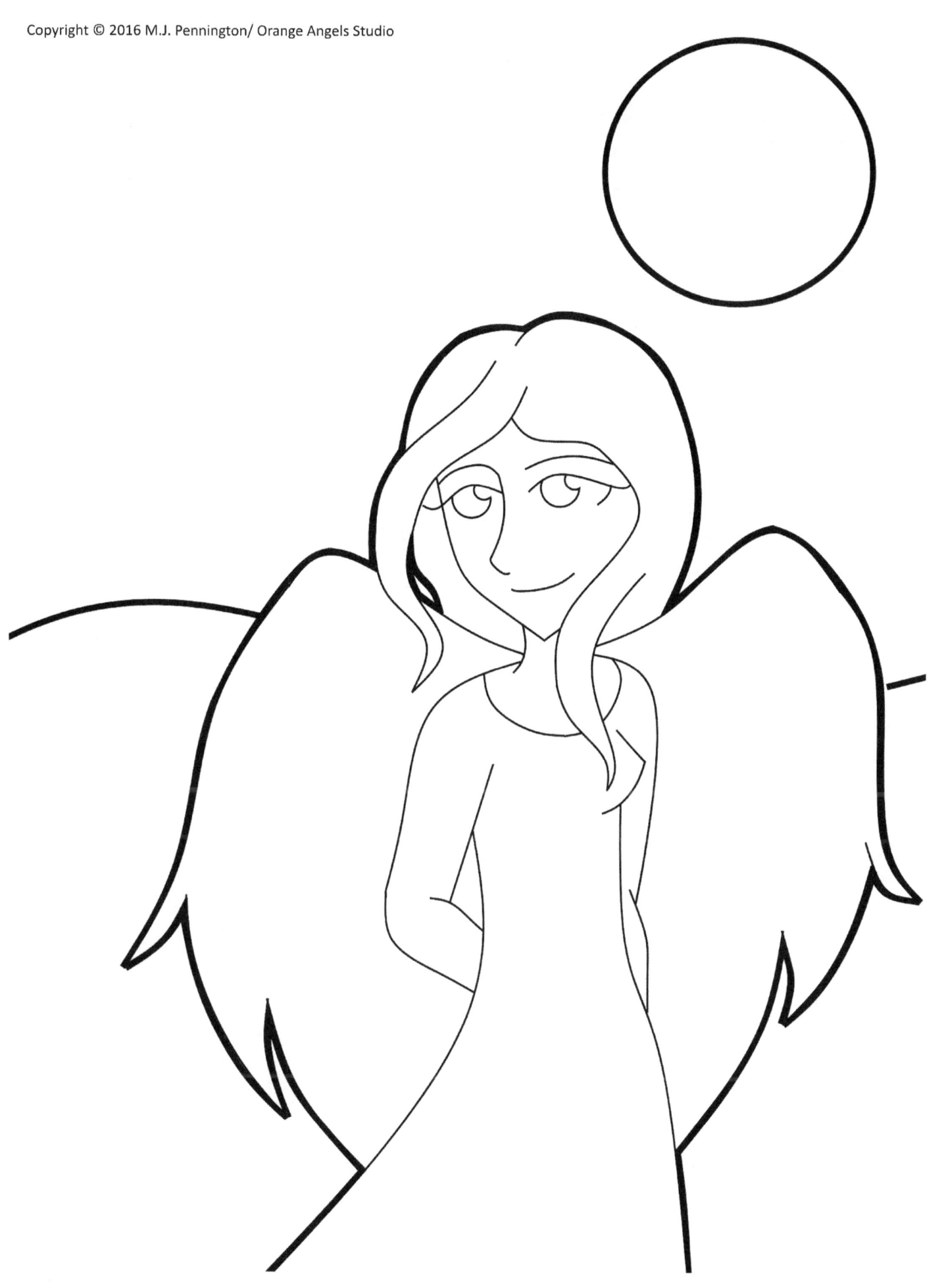

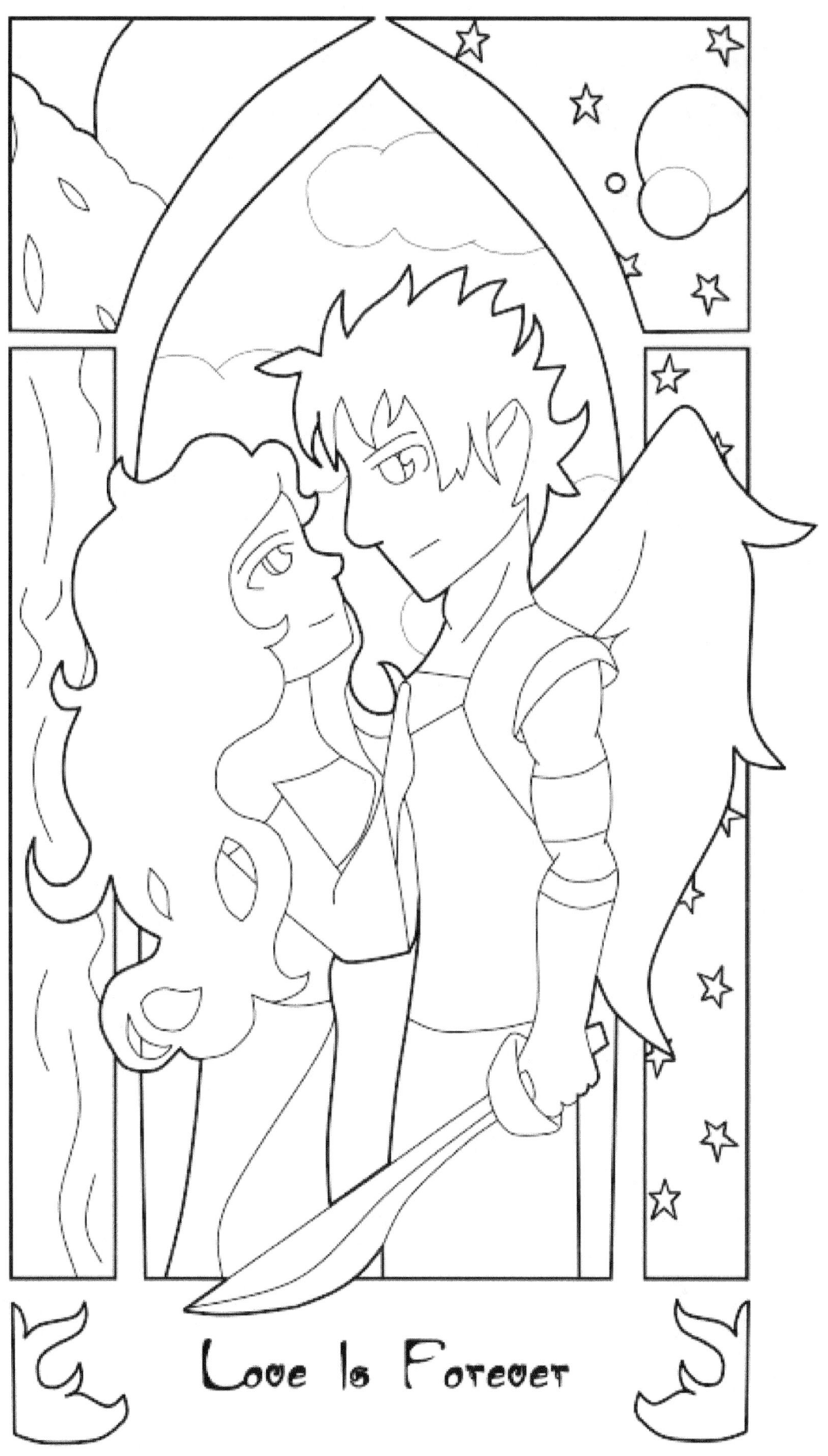

Love Is Forever

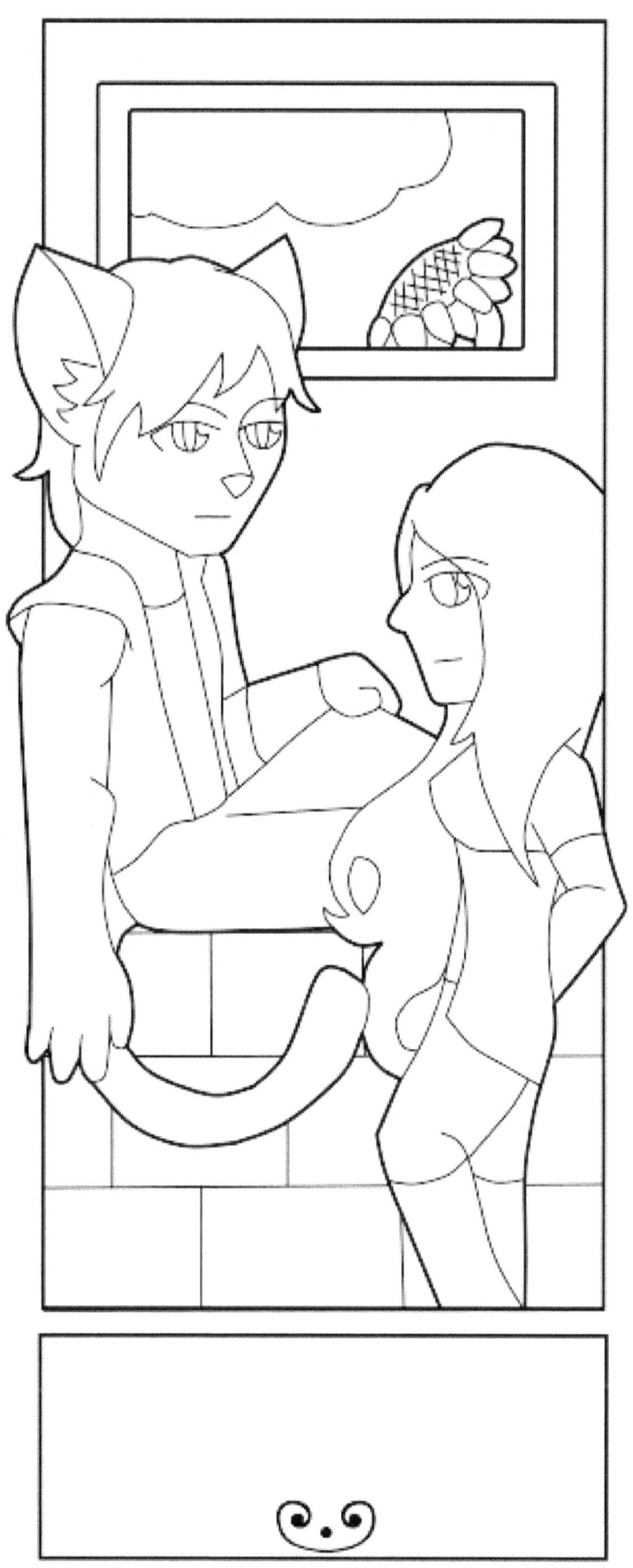

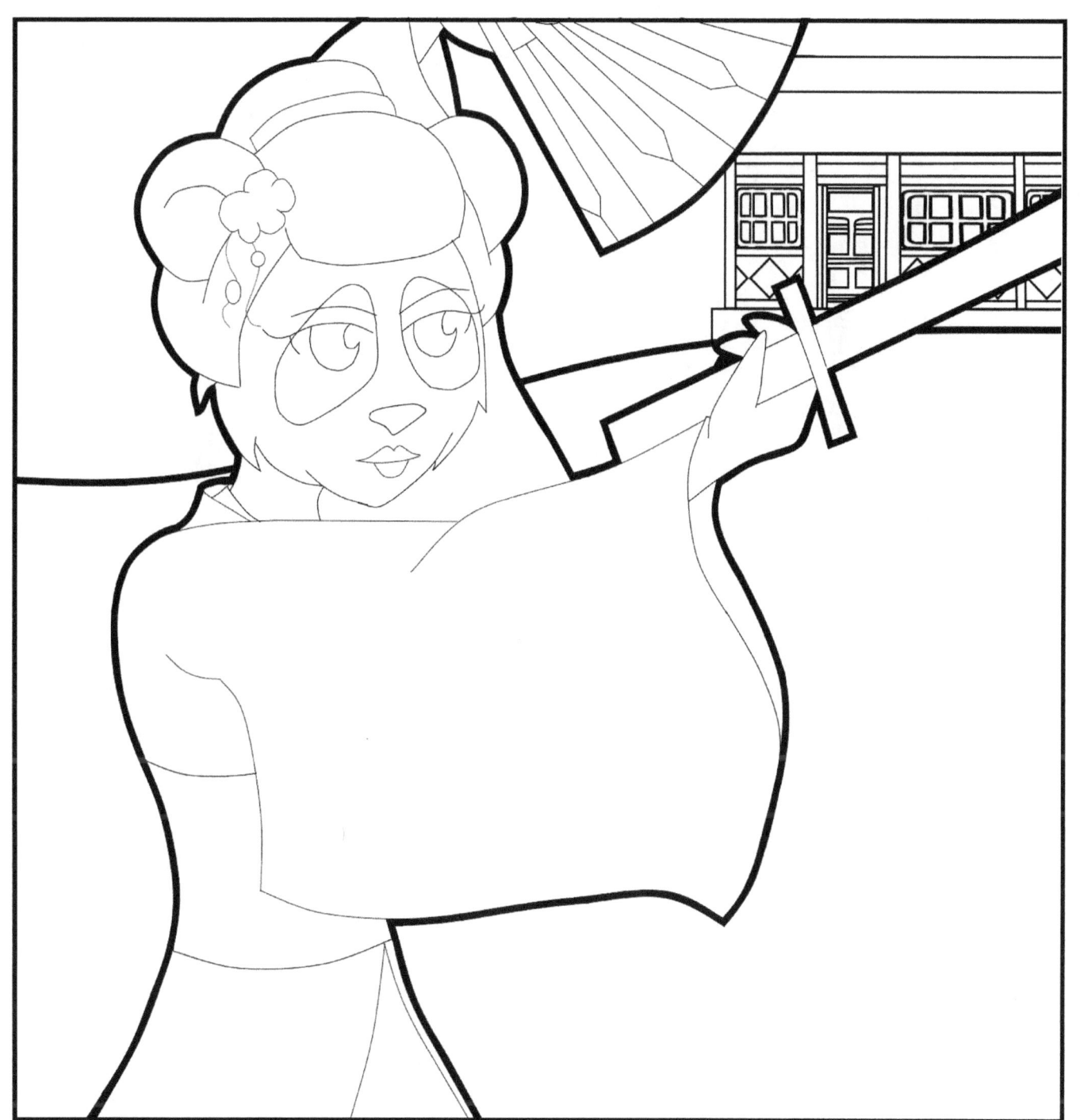

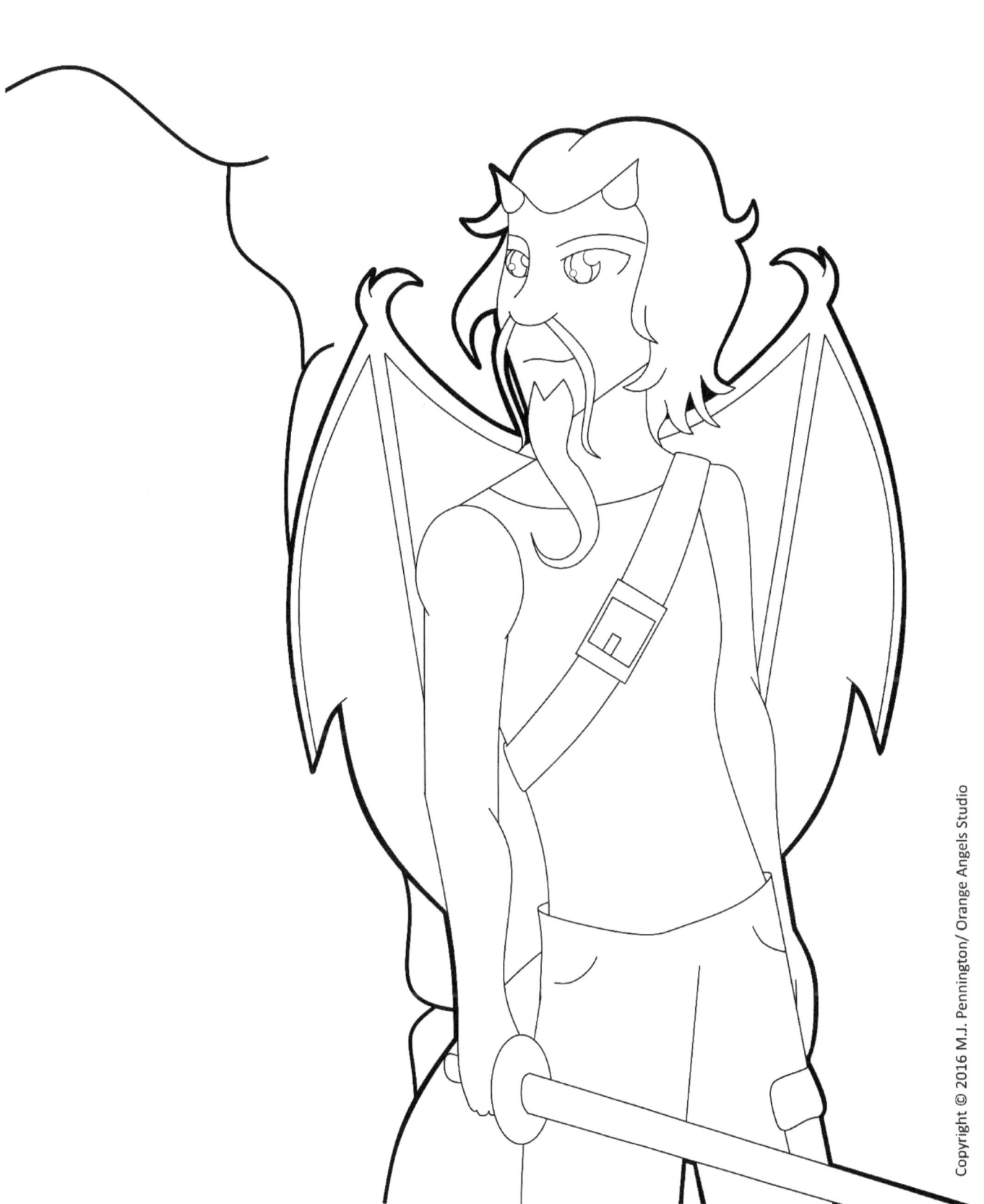

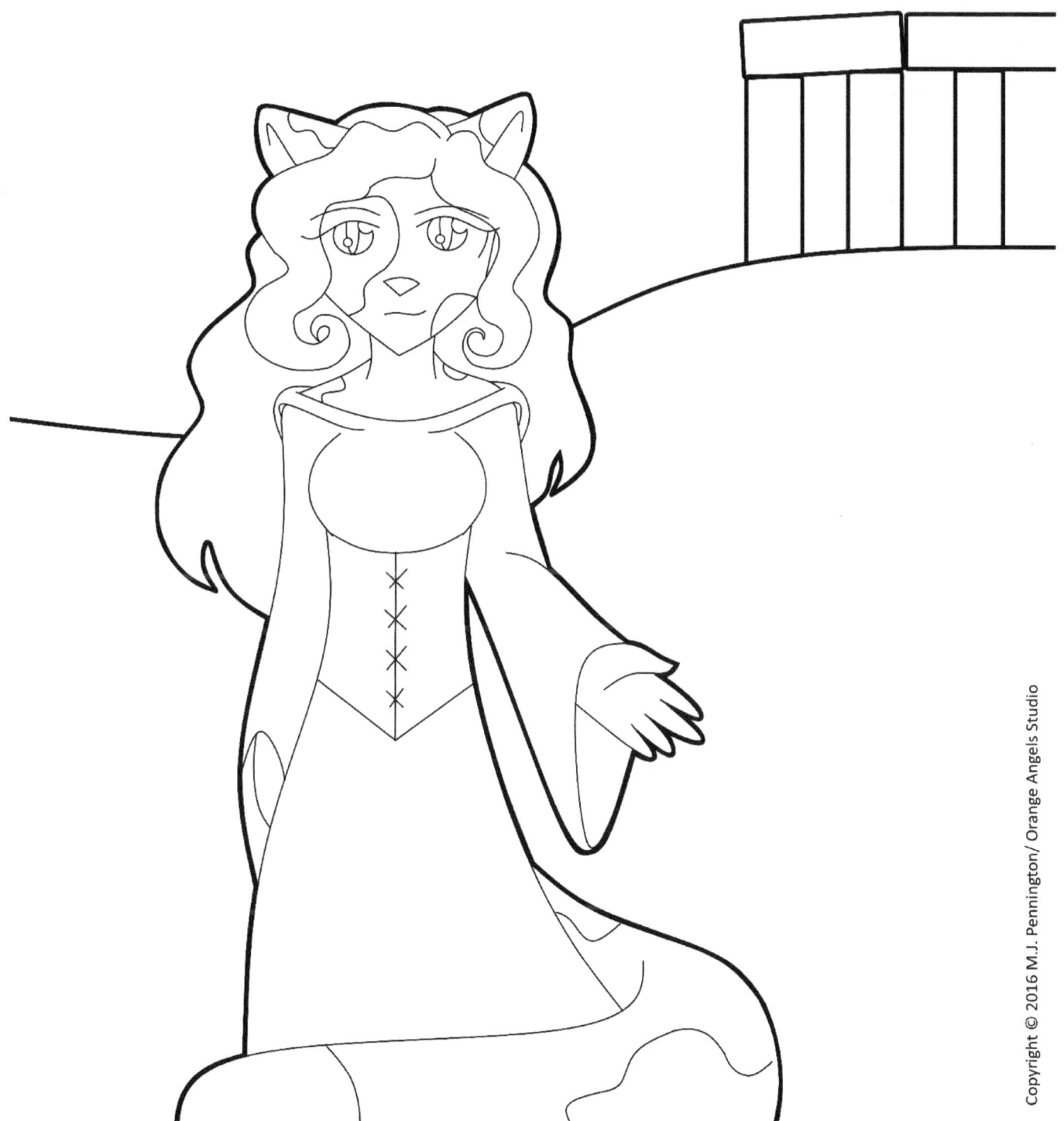

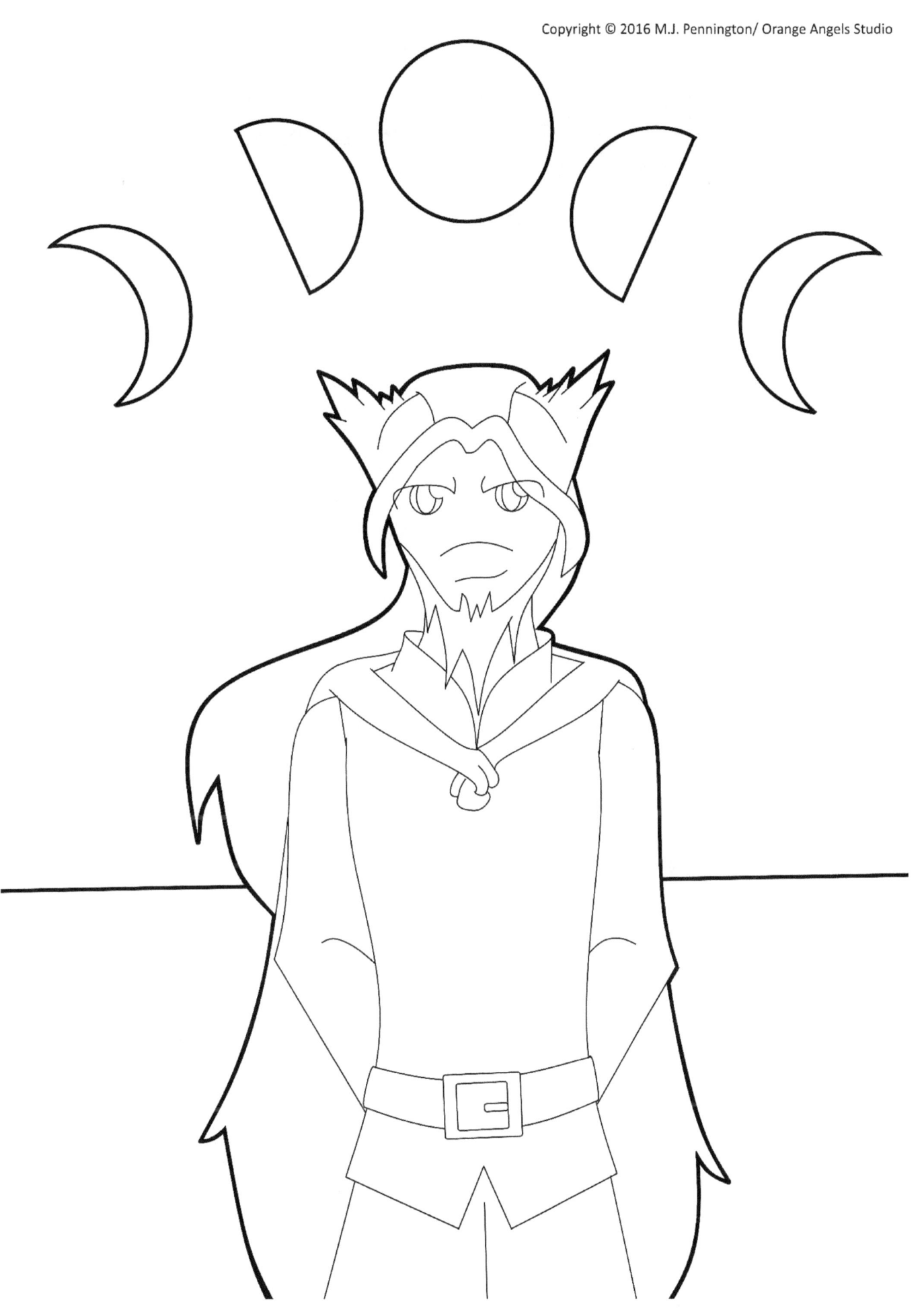

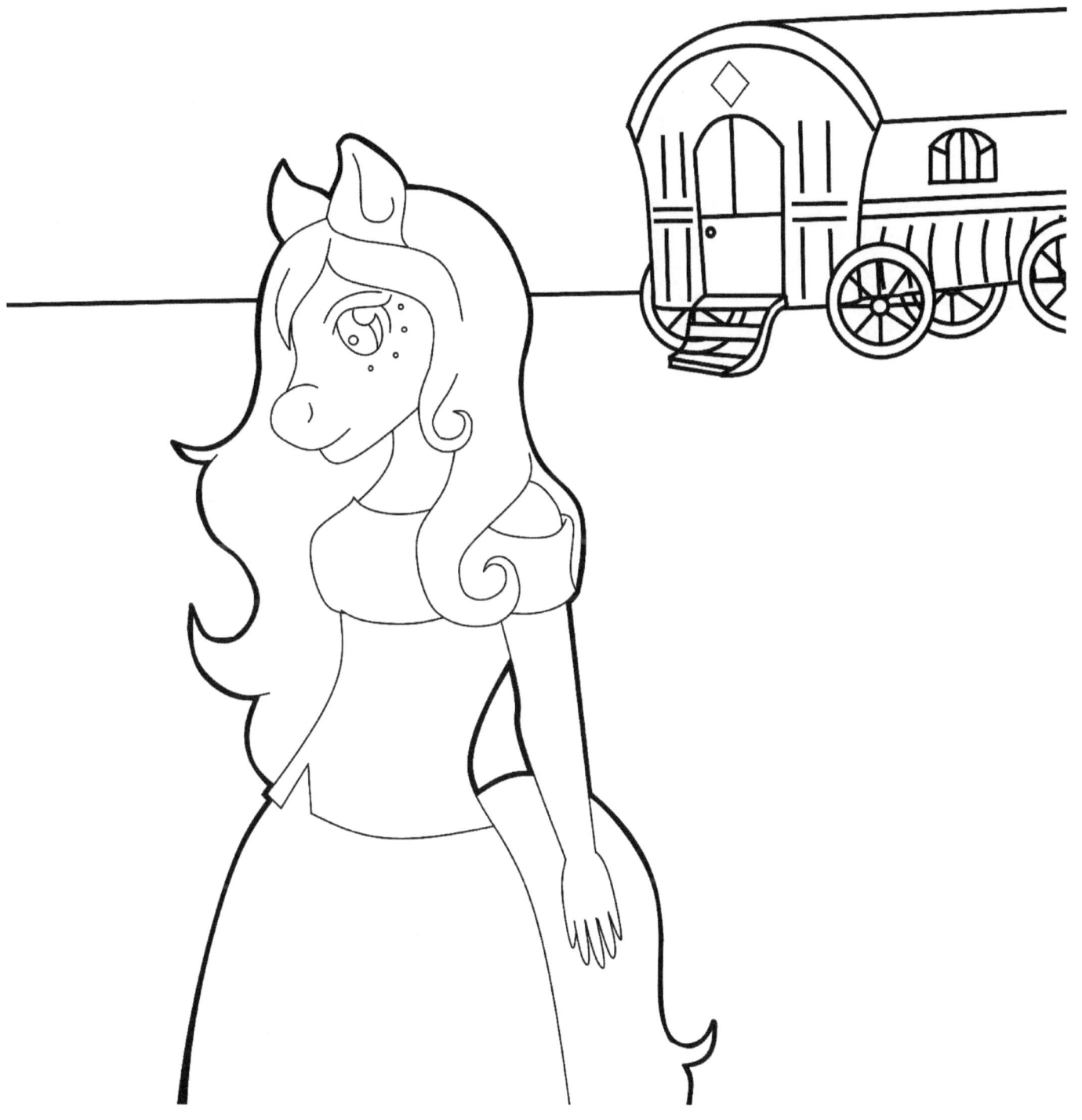

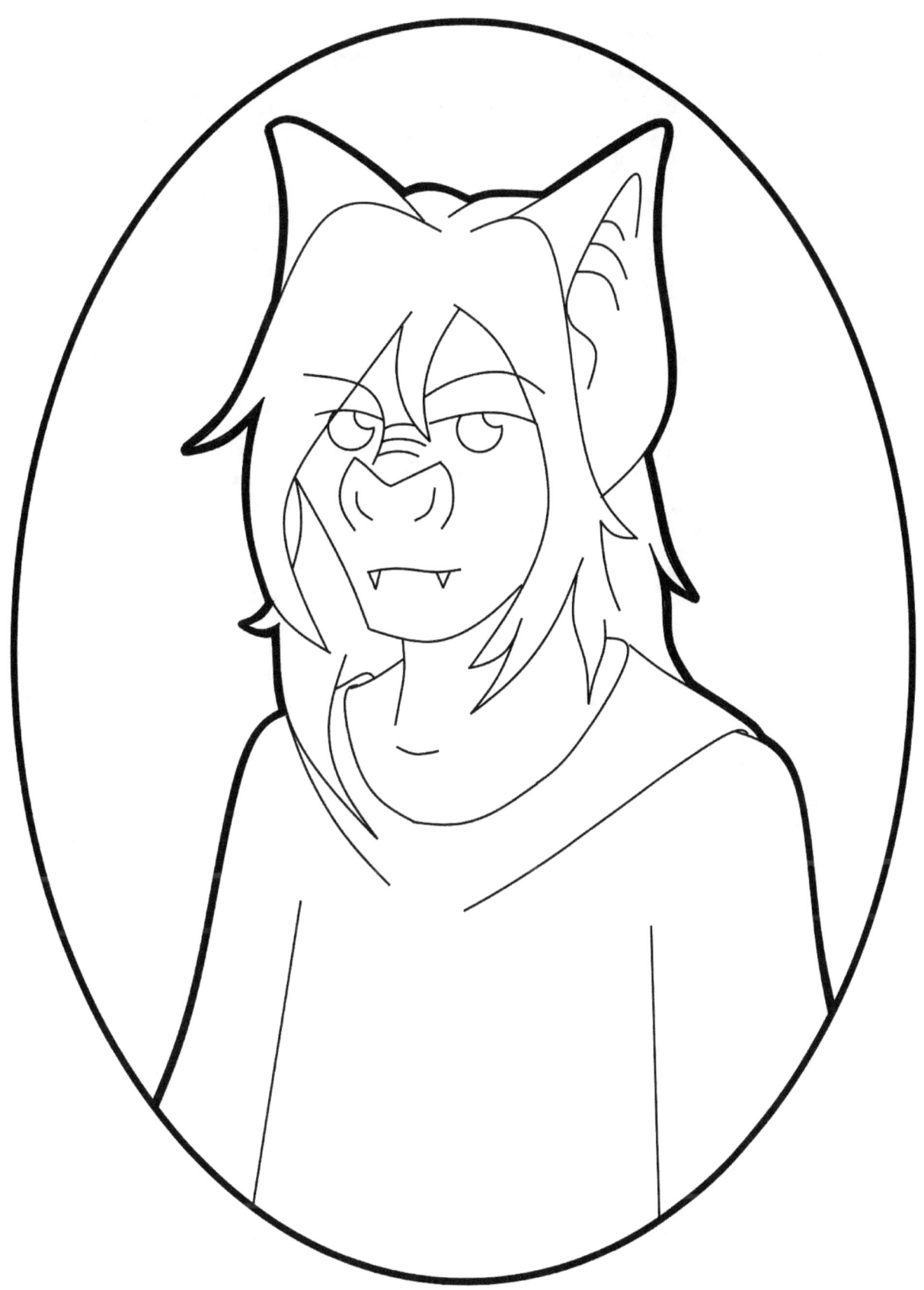

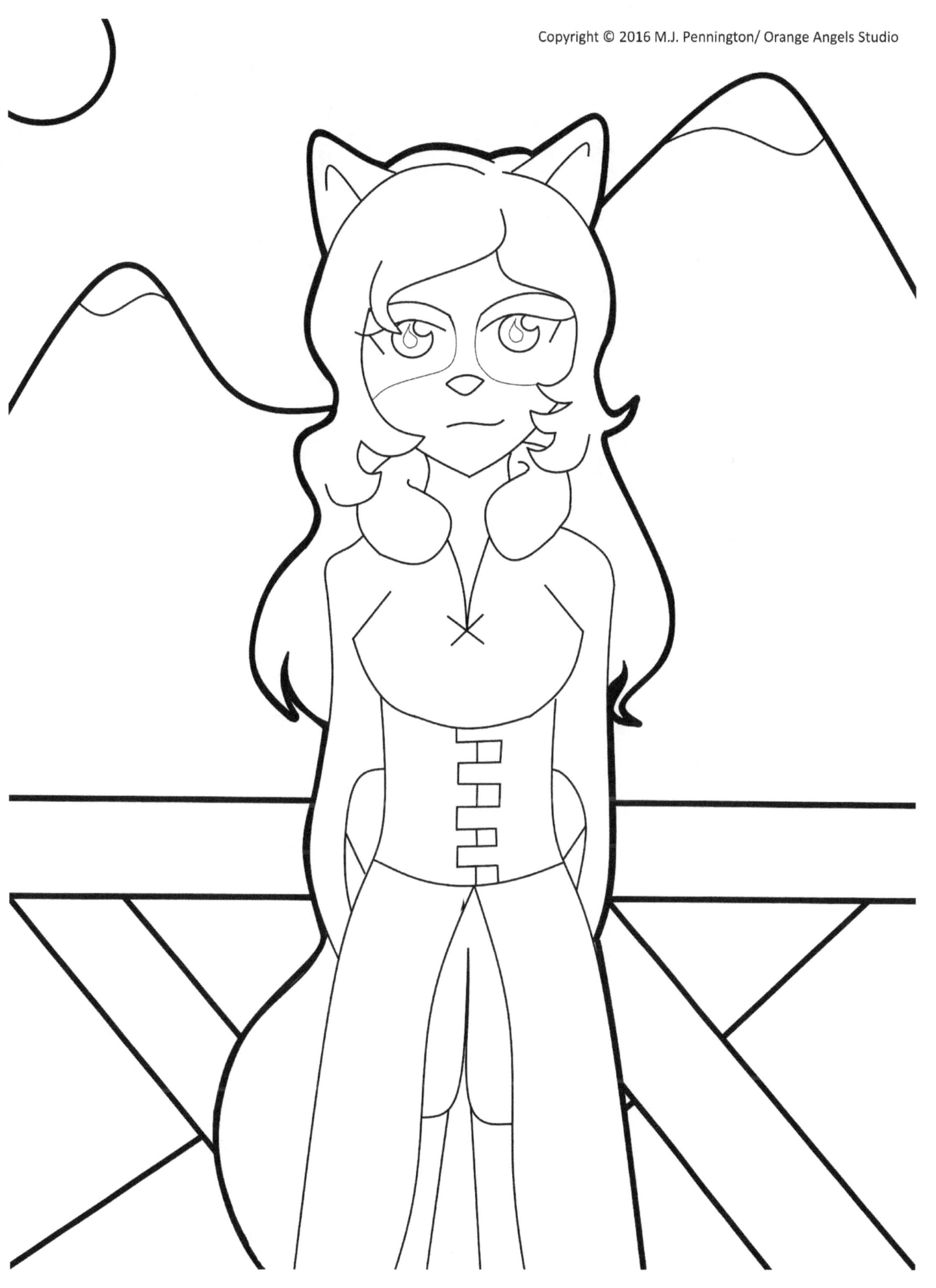

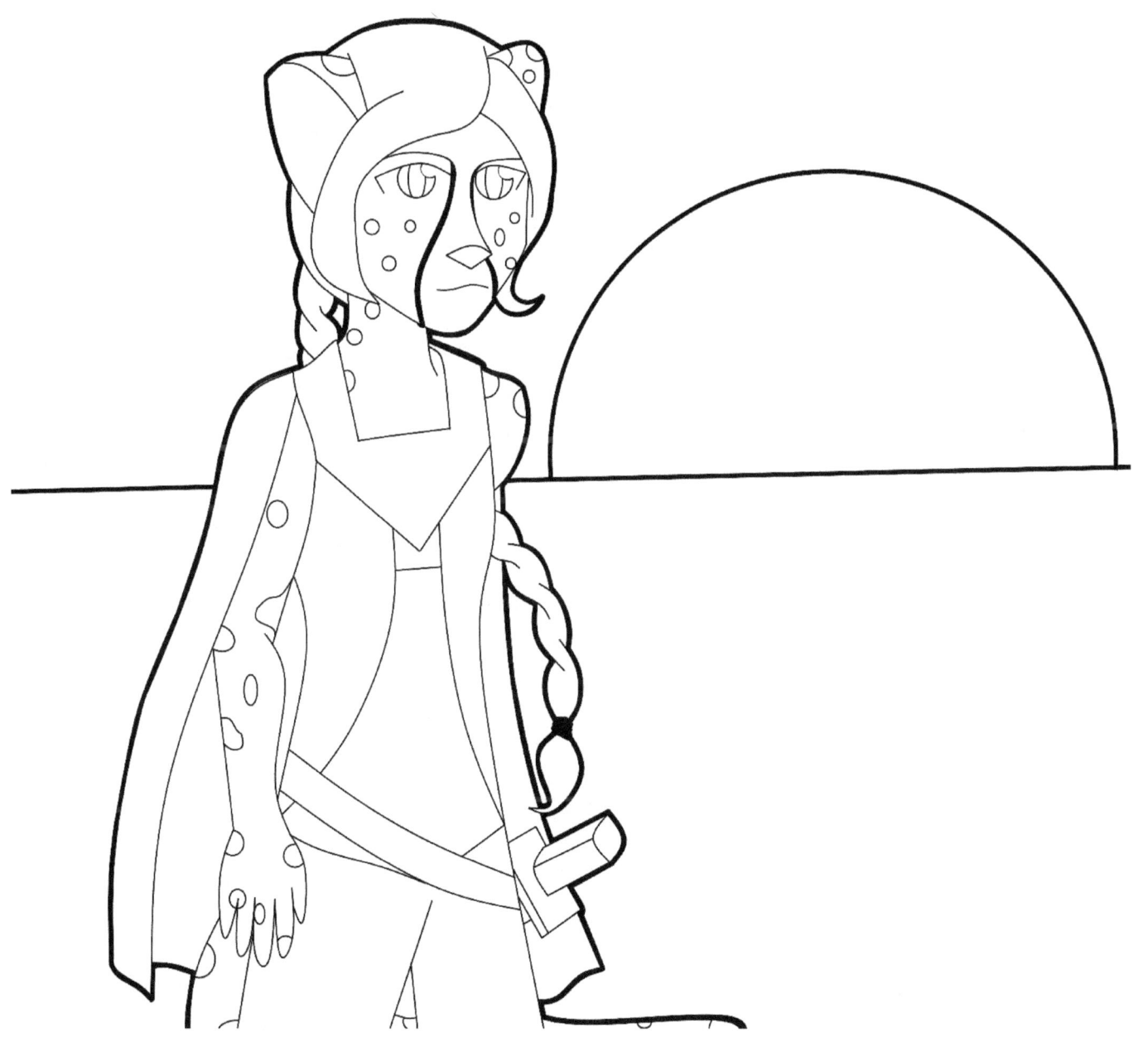

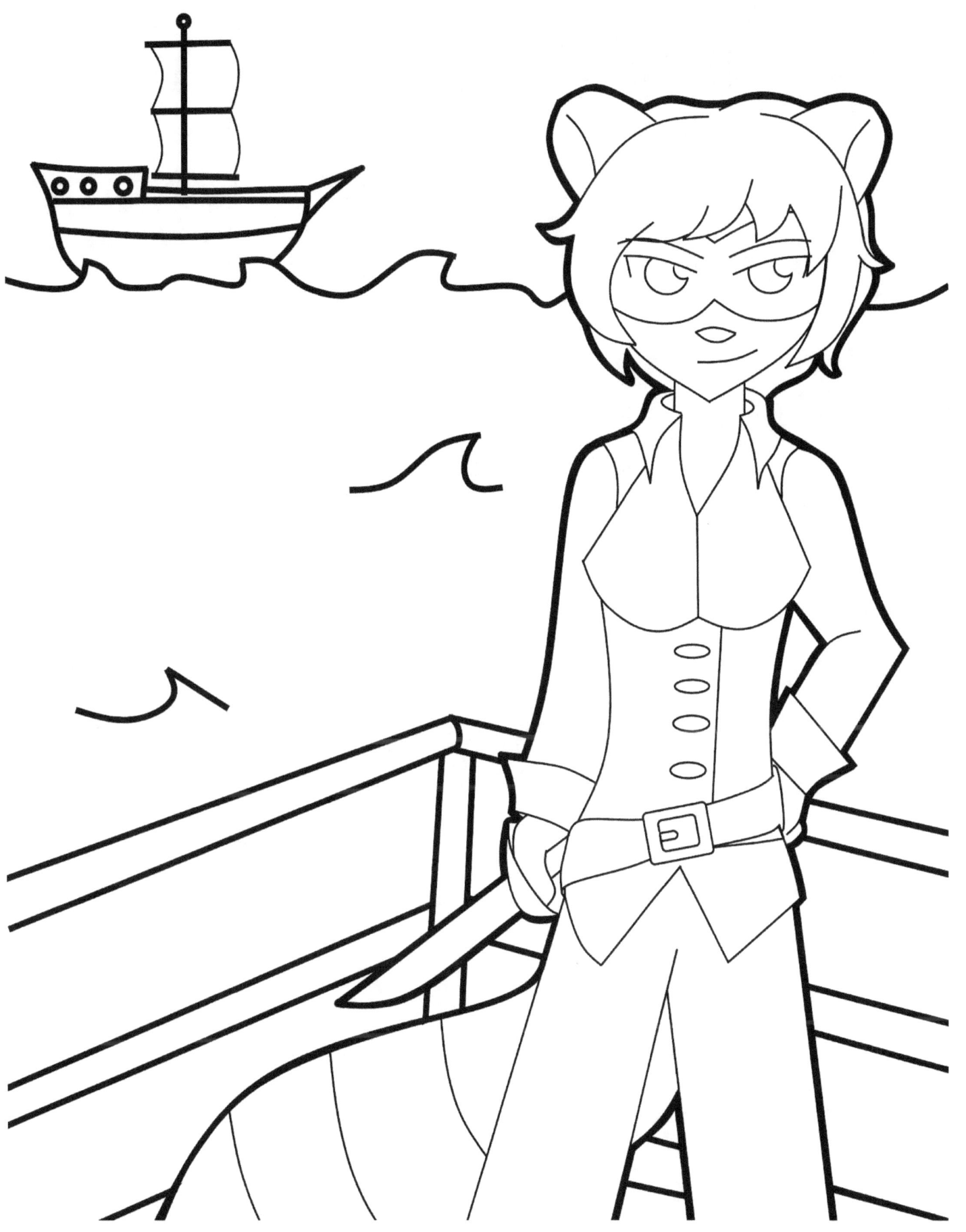

THE HERMIT

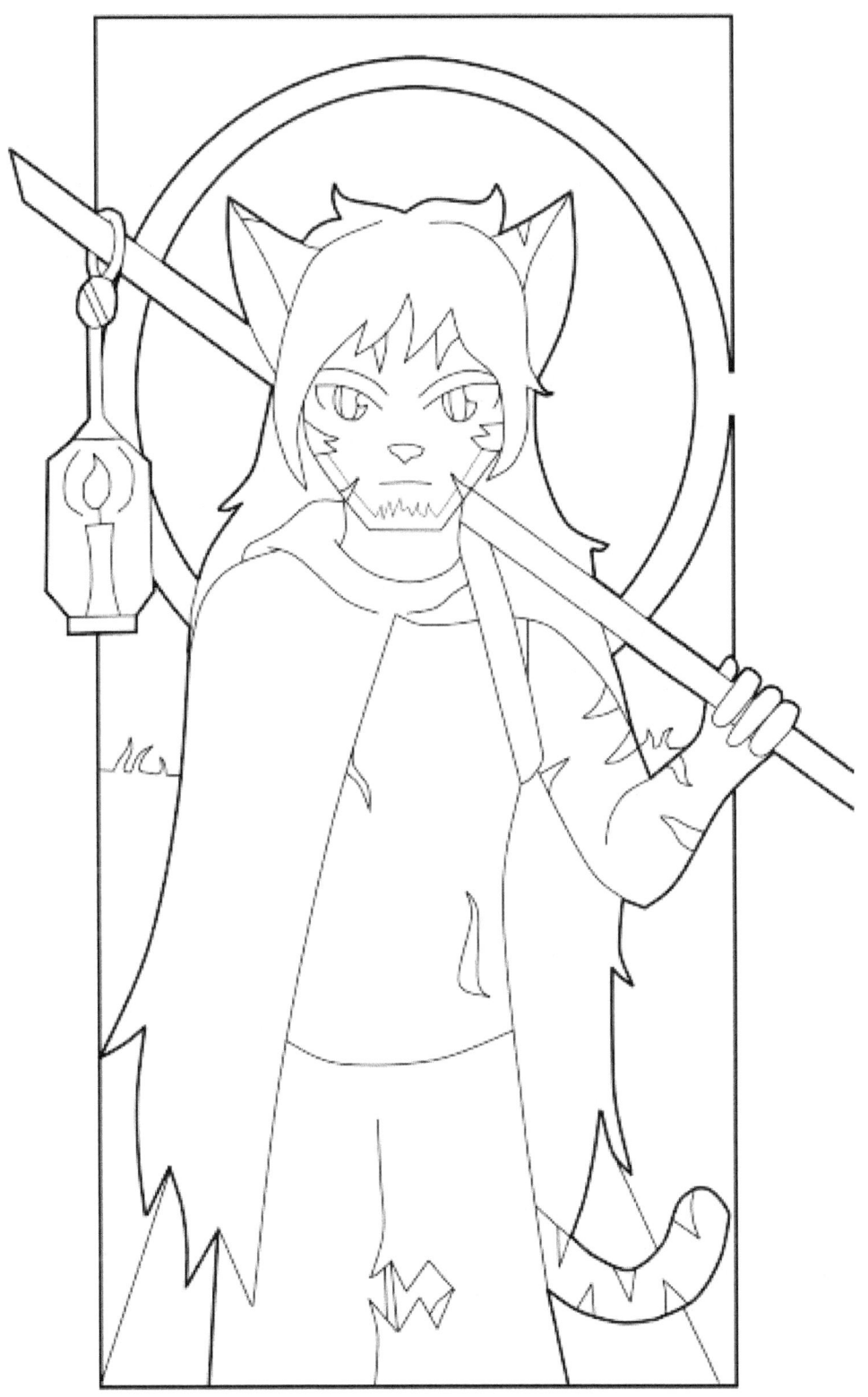

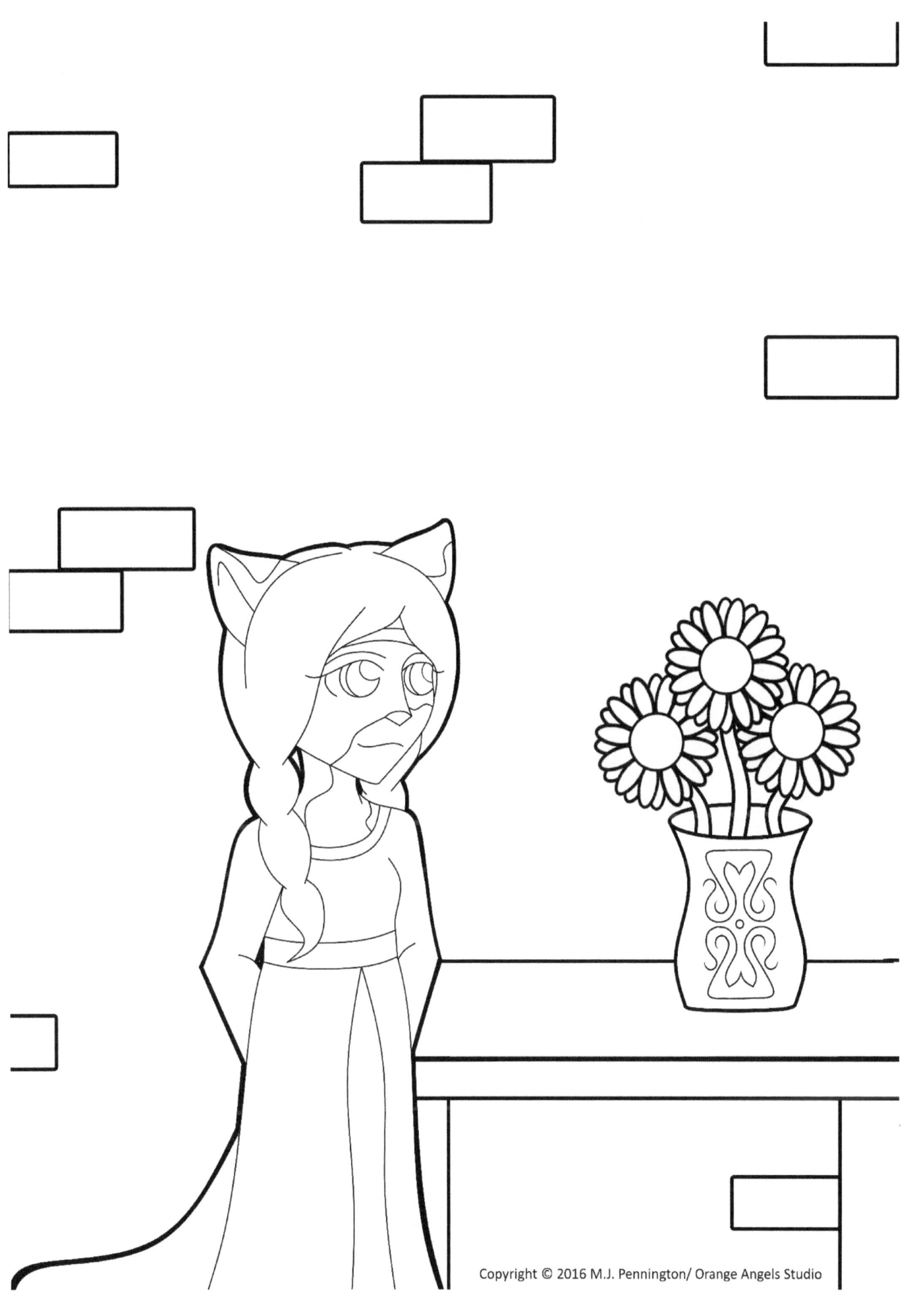

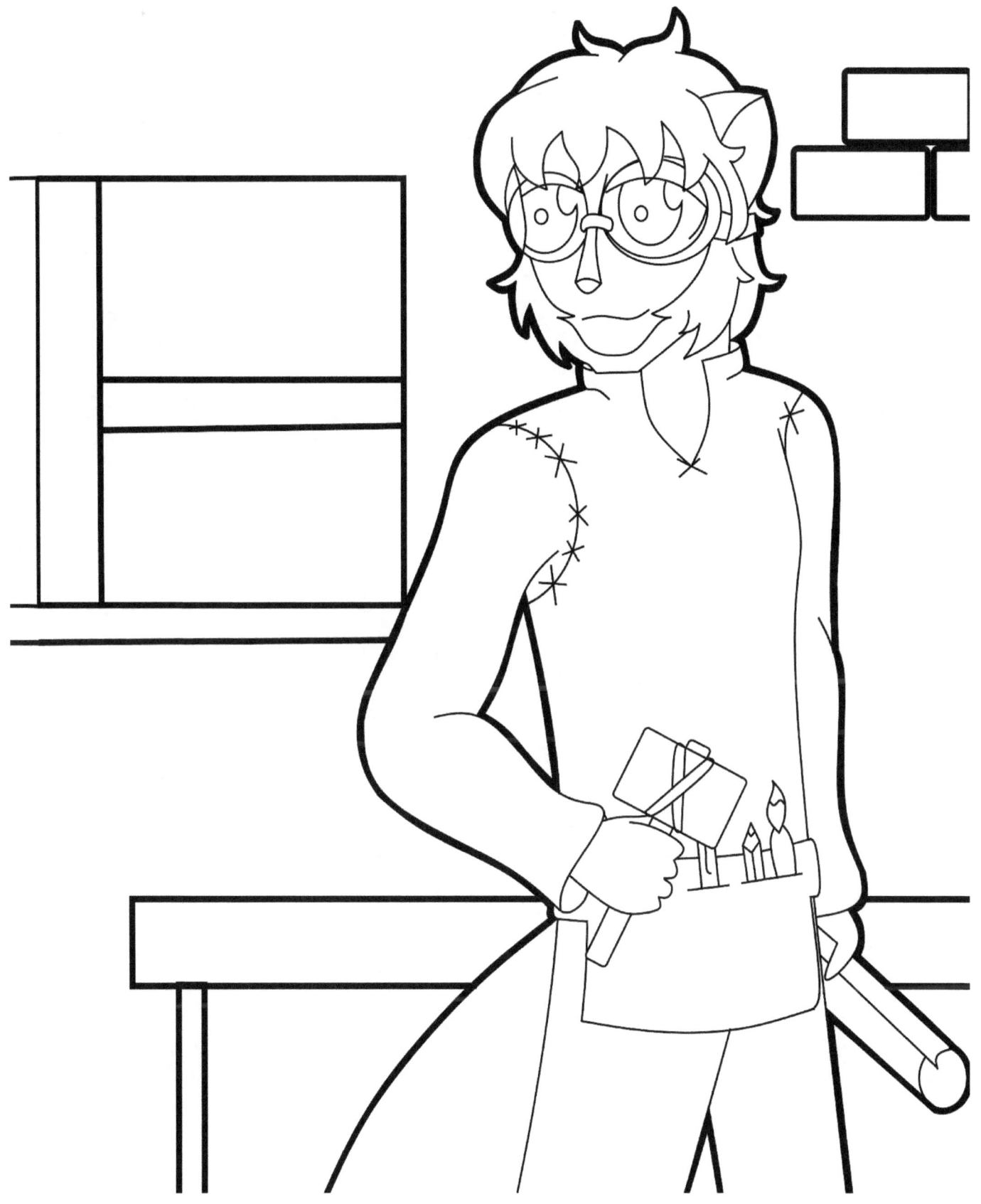

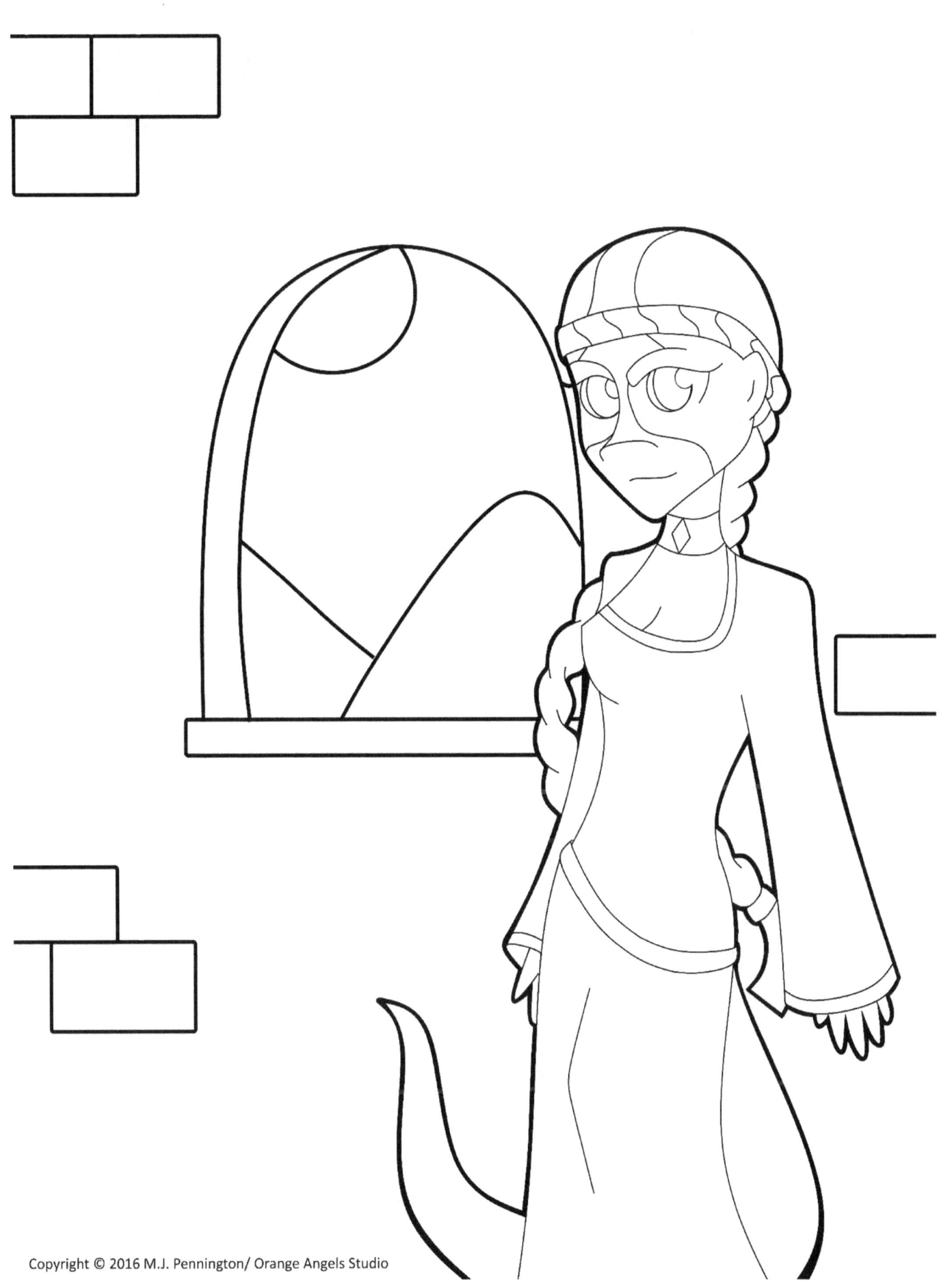

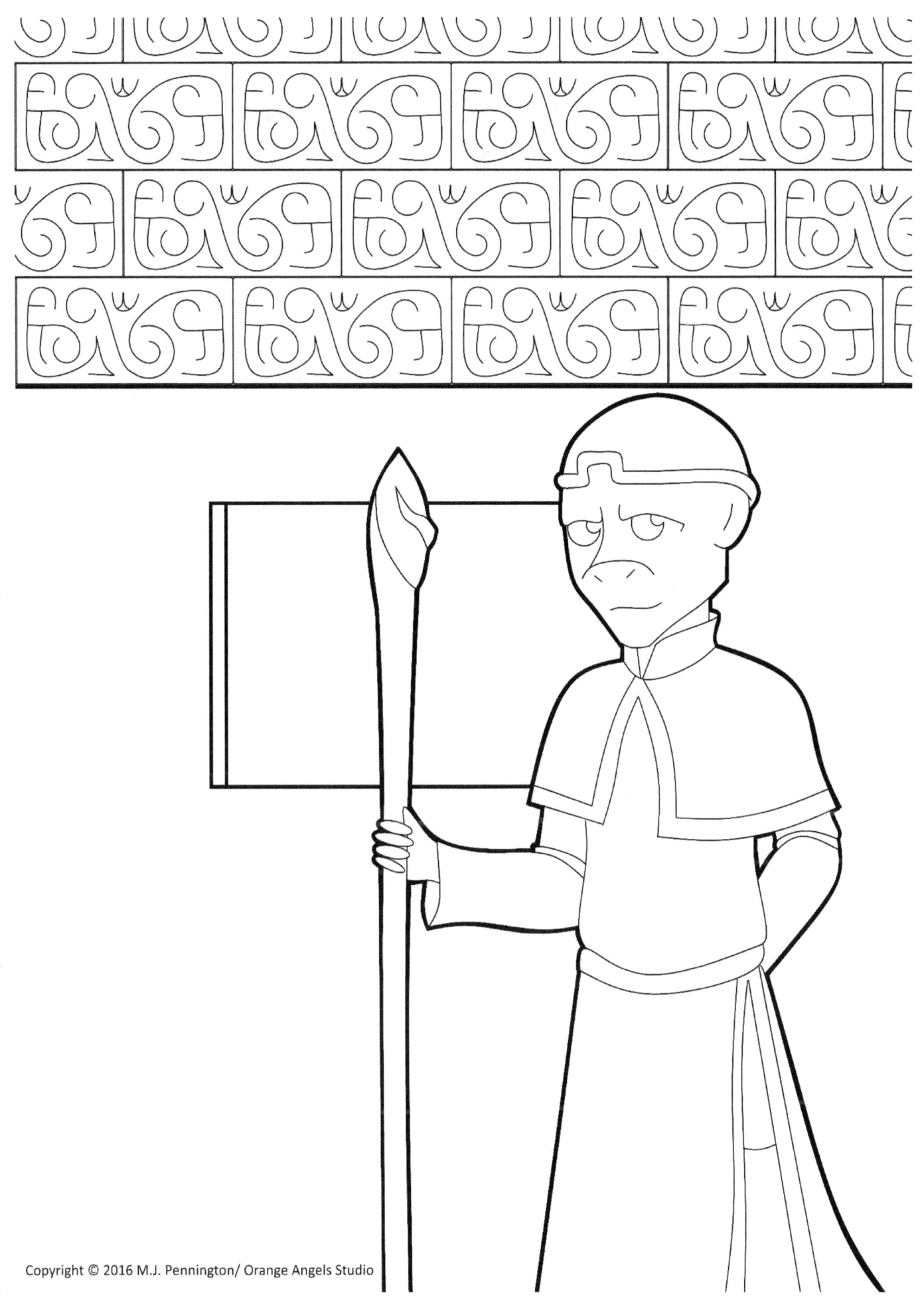

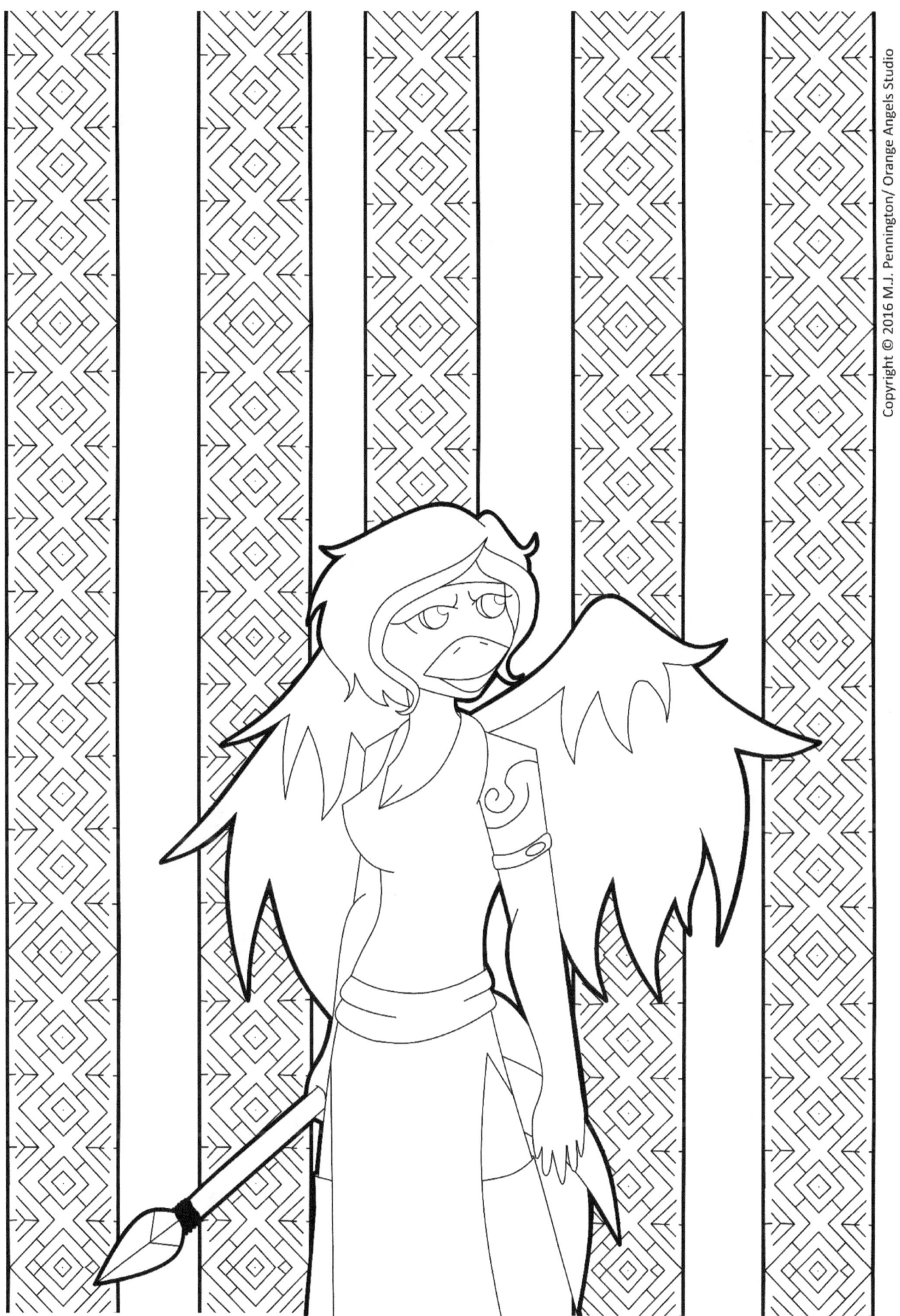

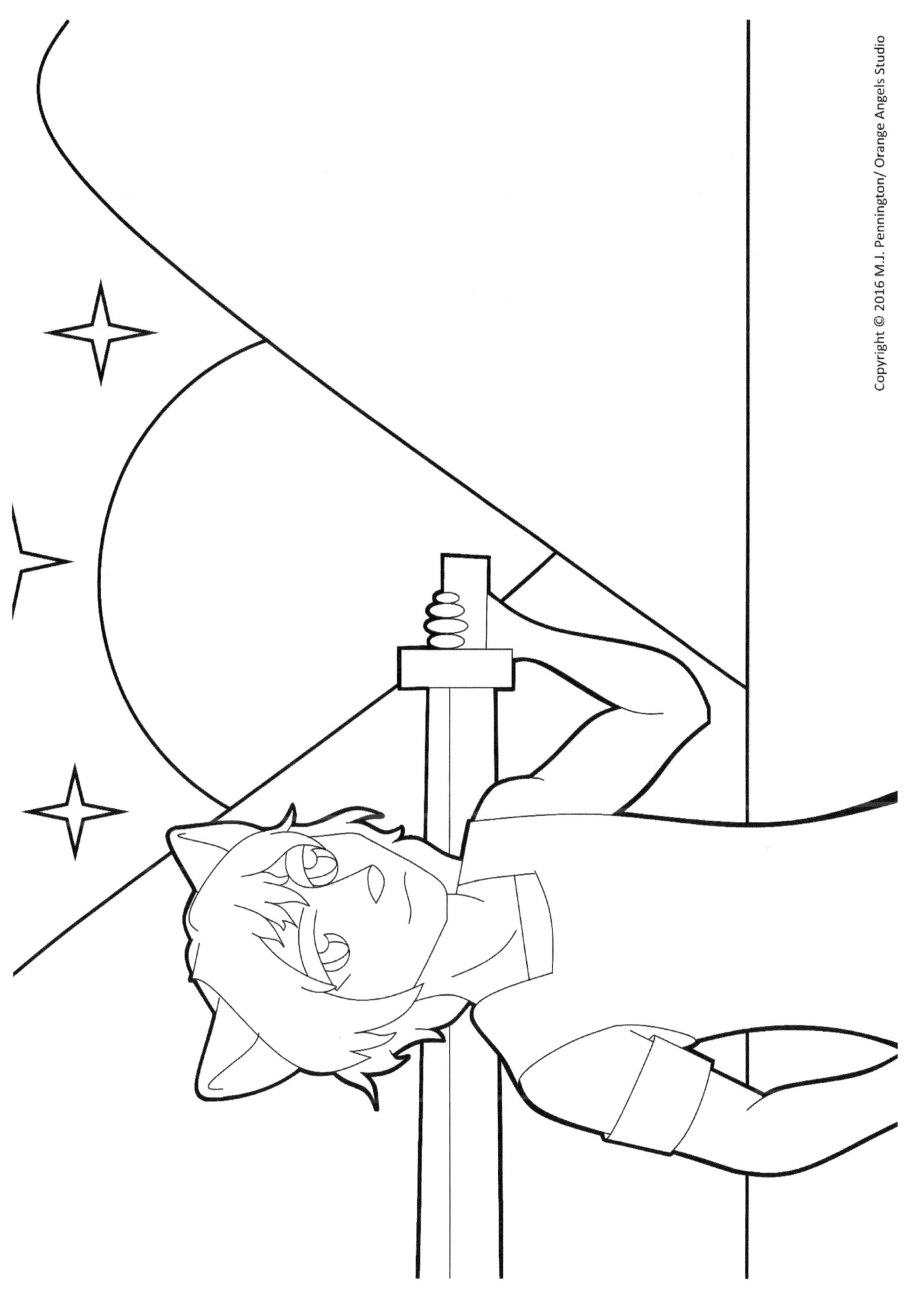

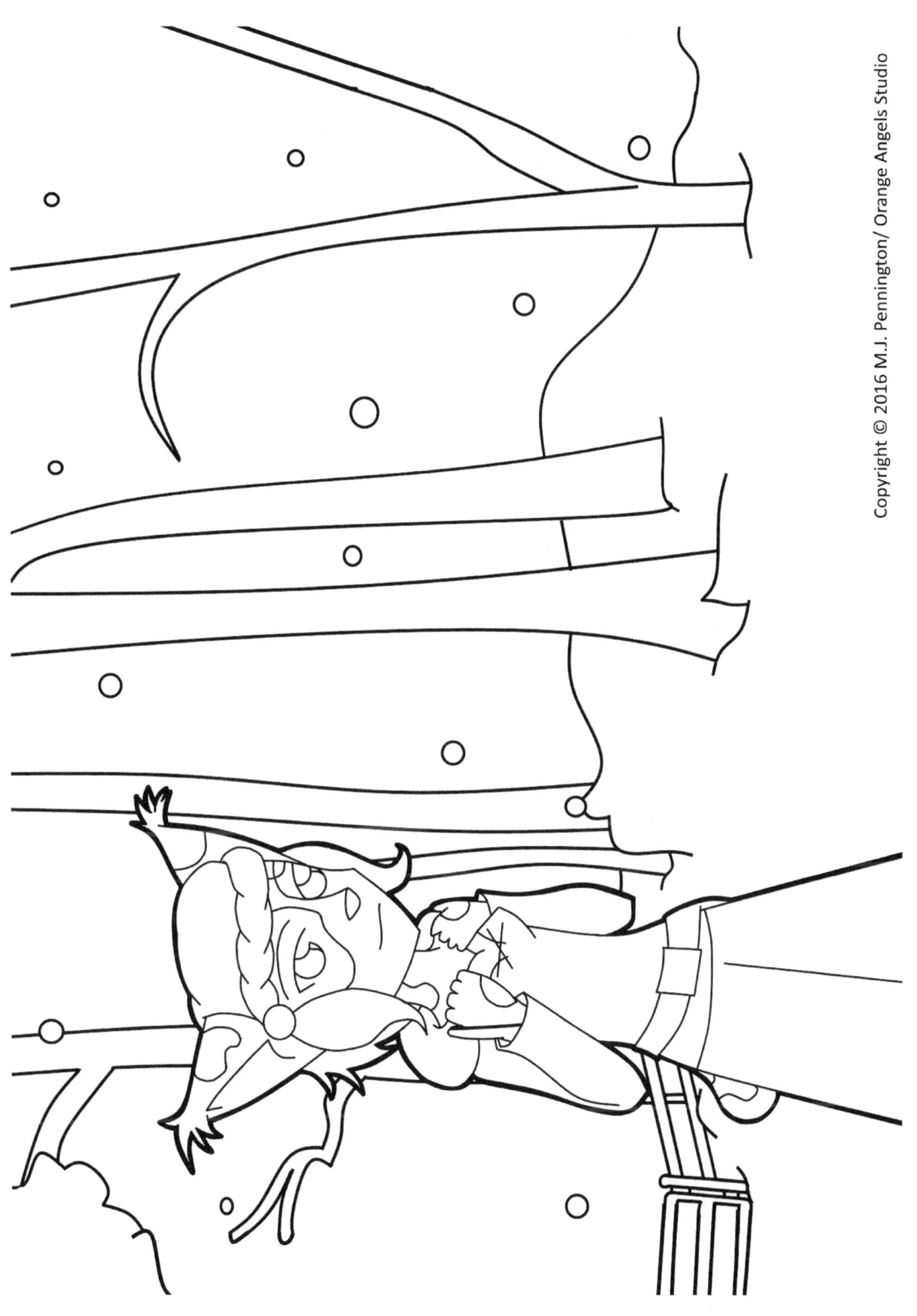

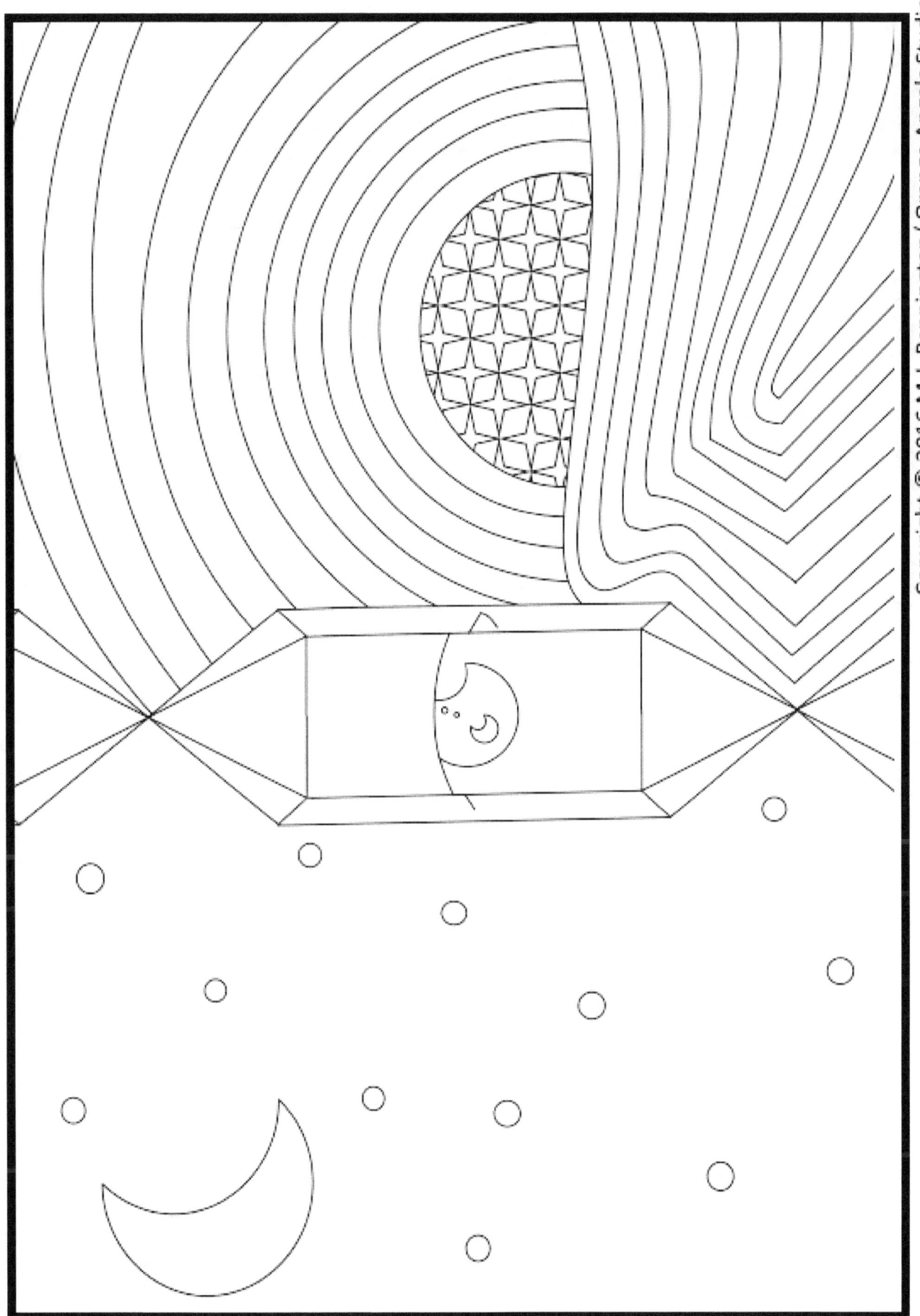

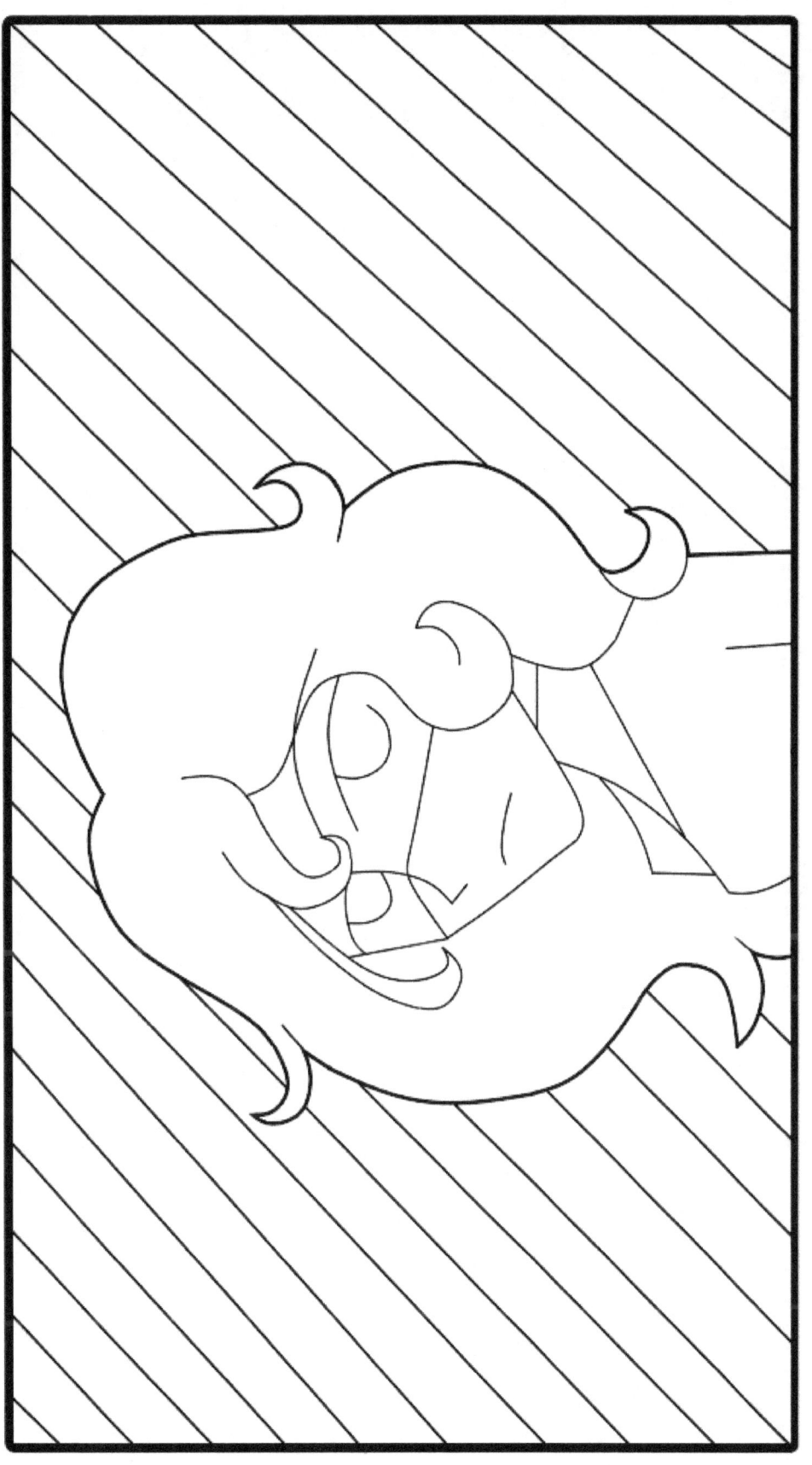

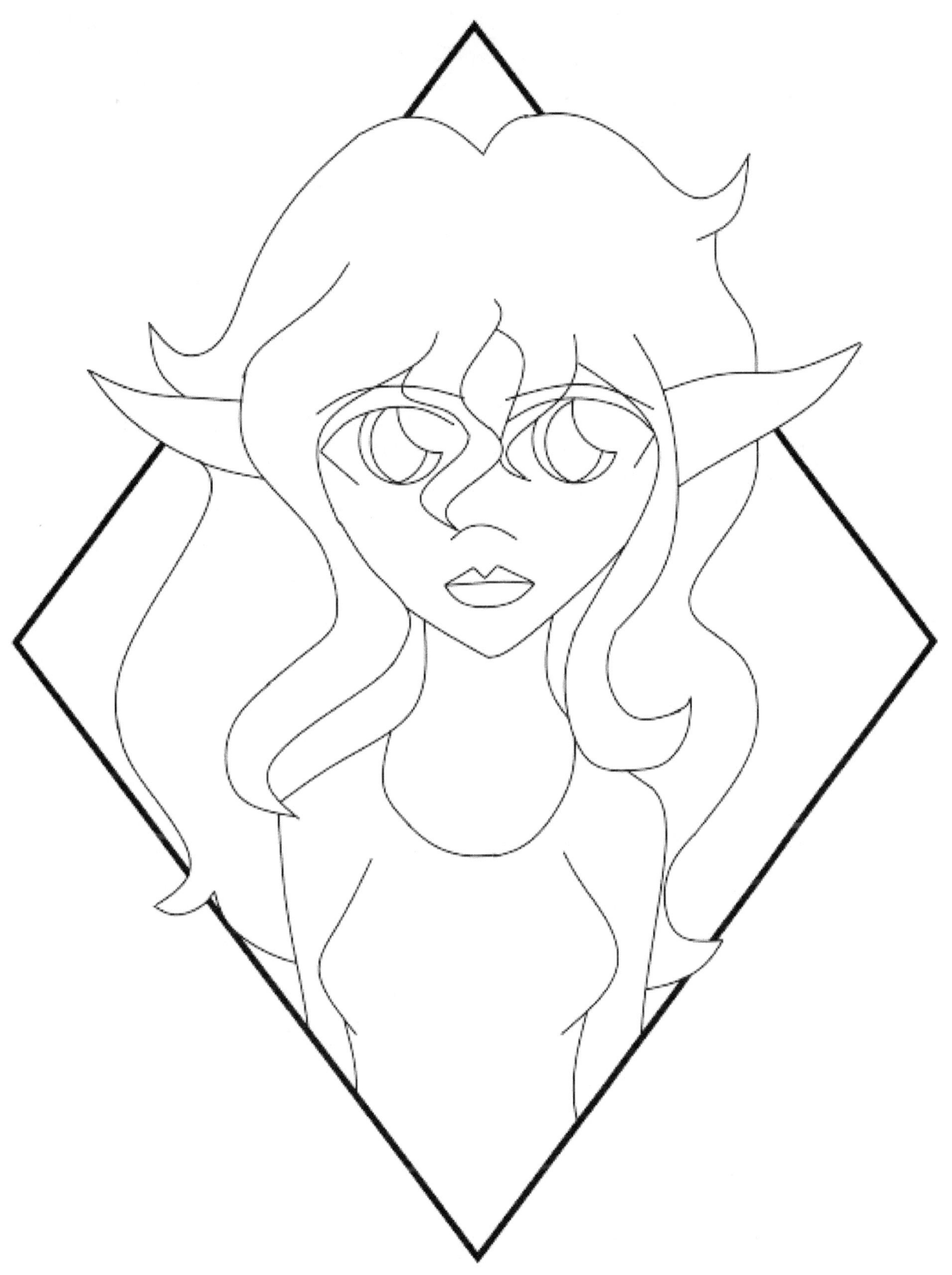

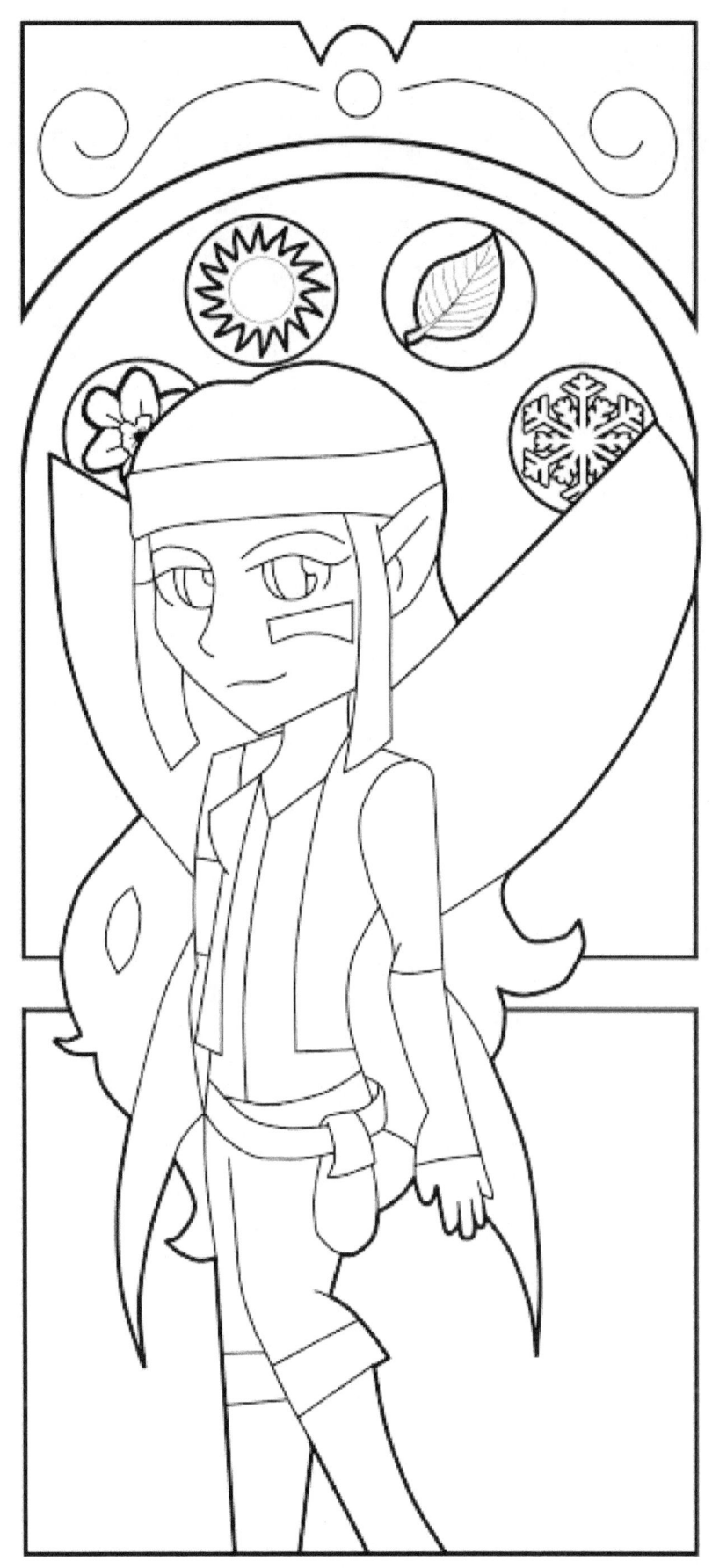

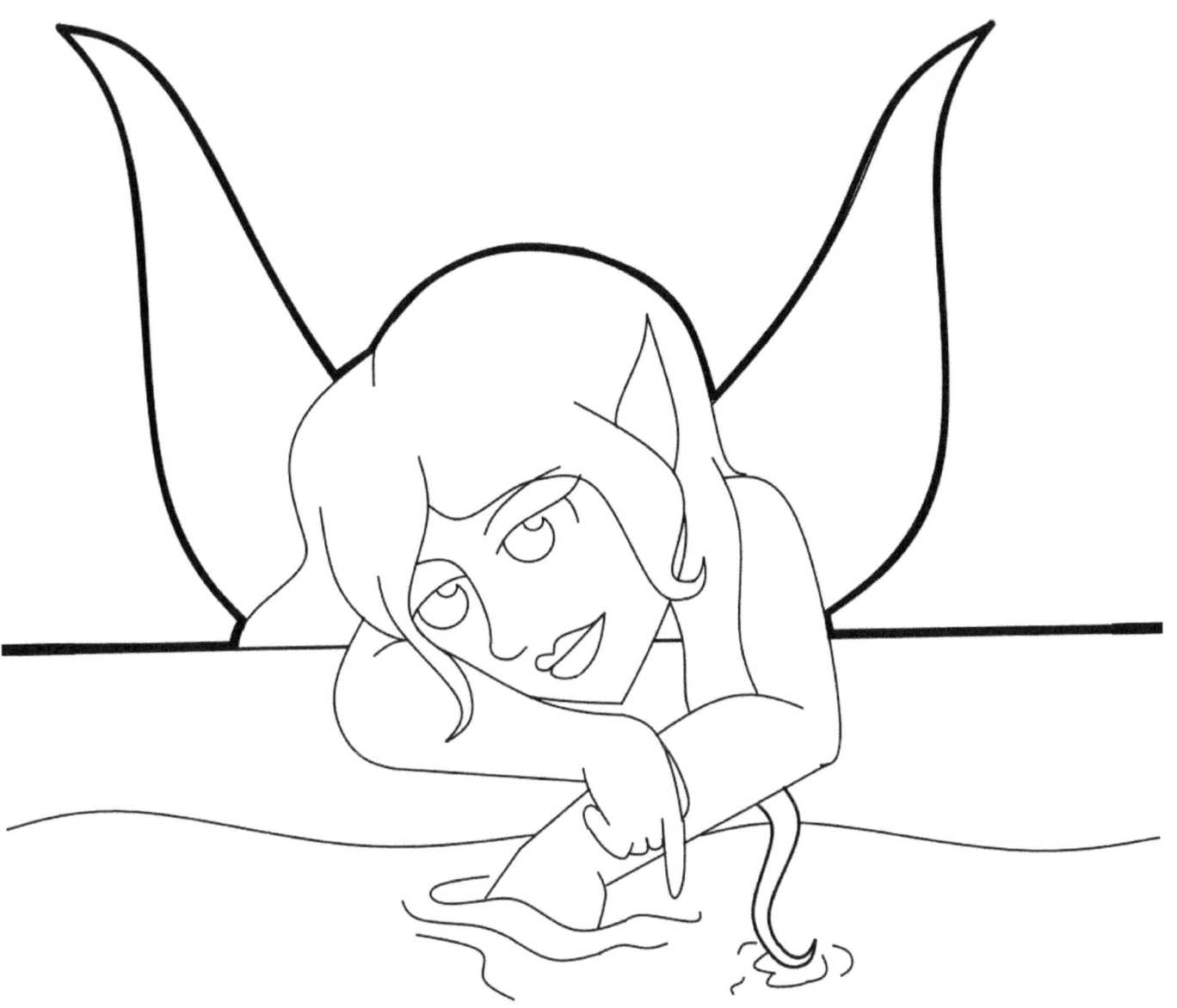

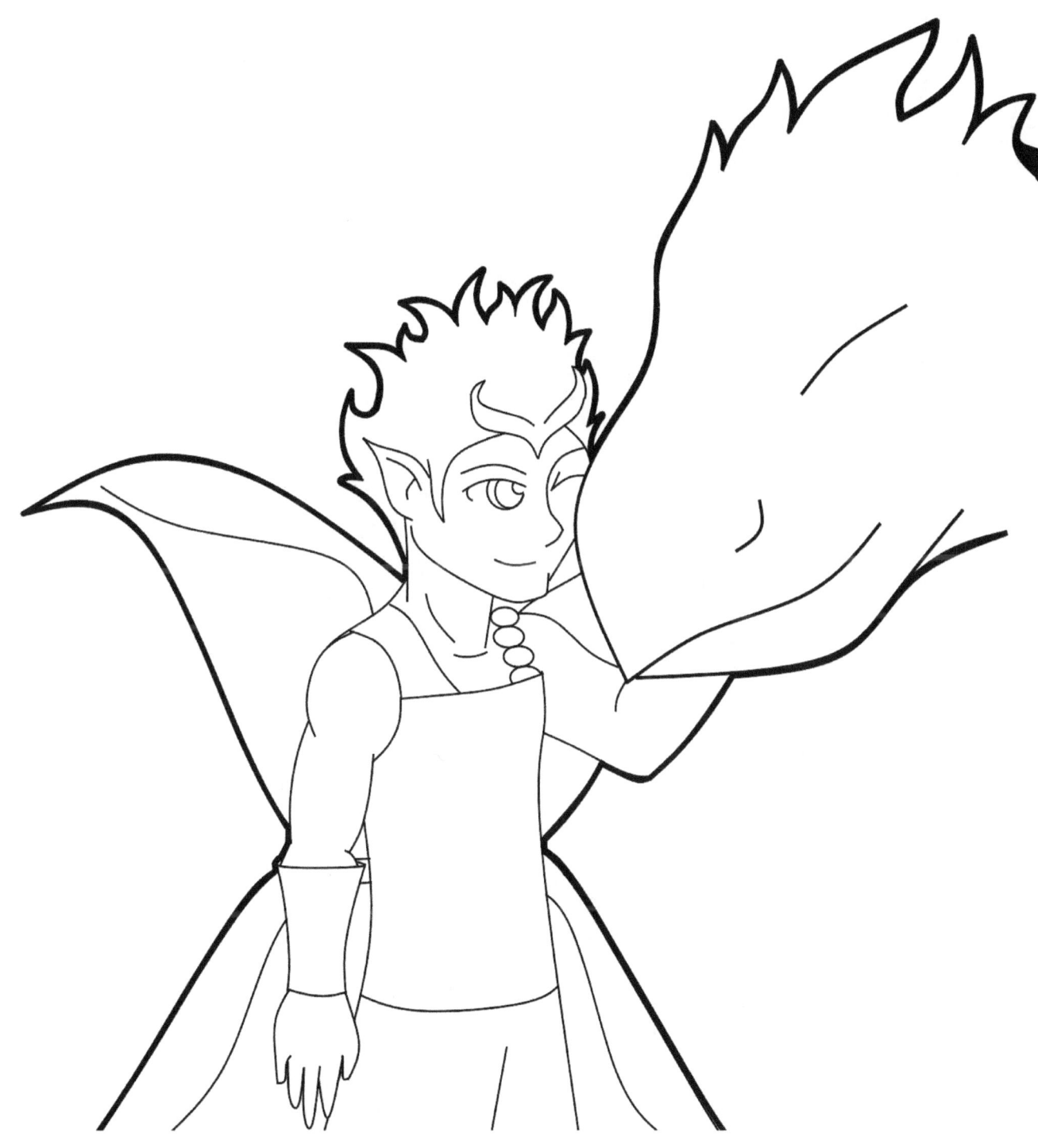

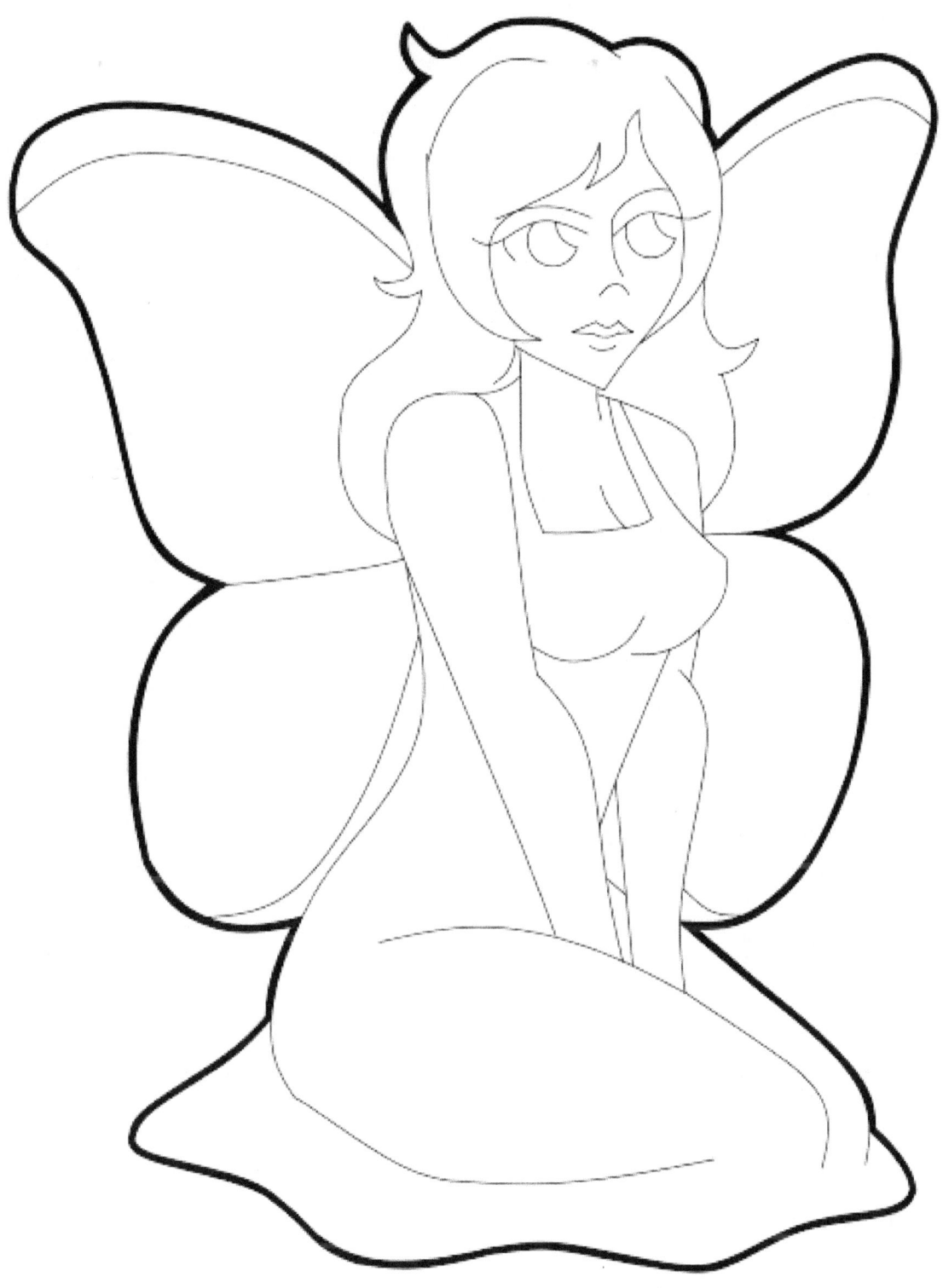

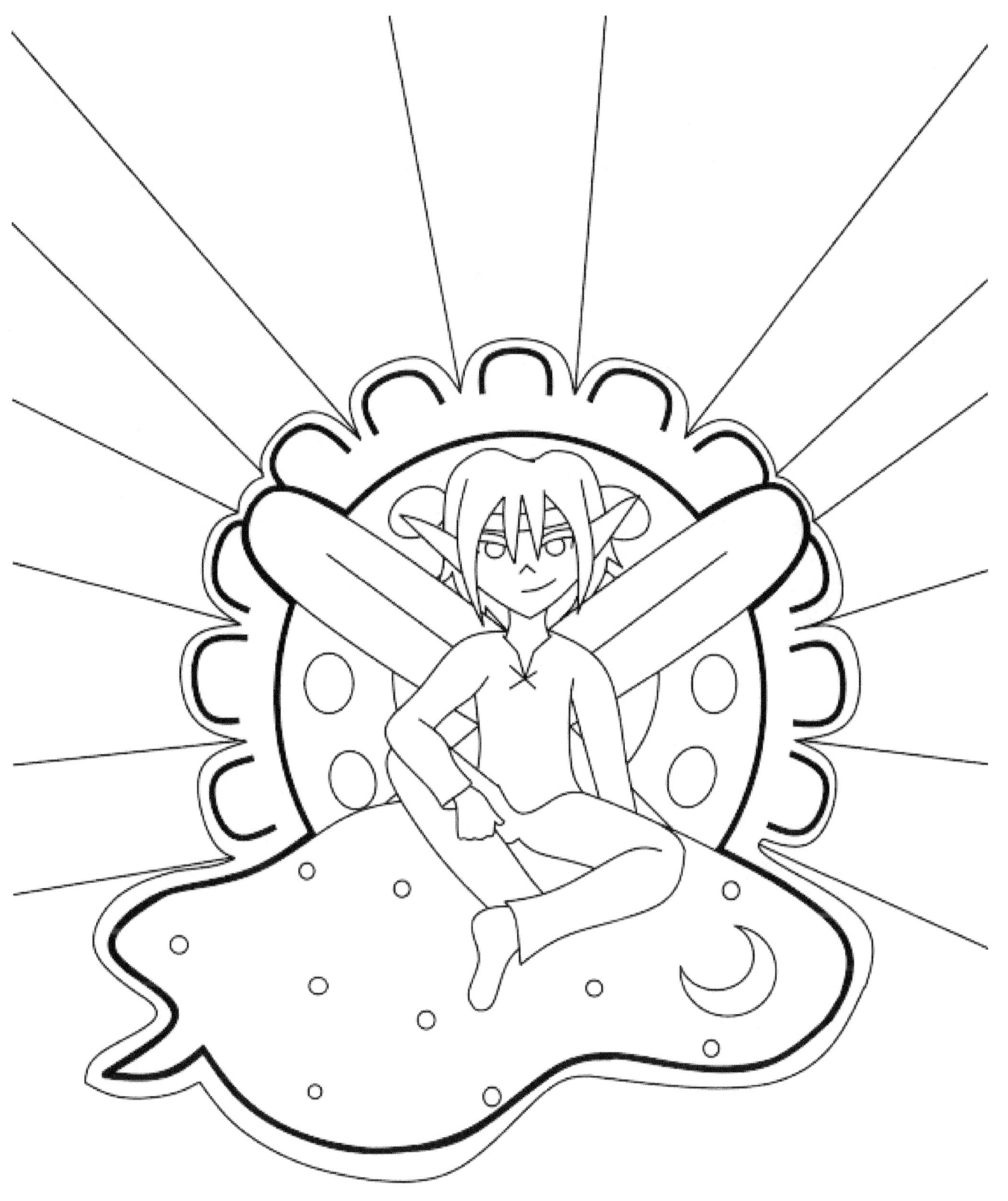

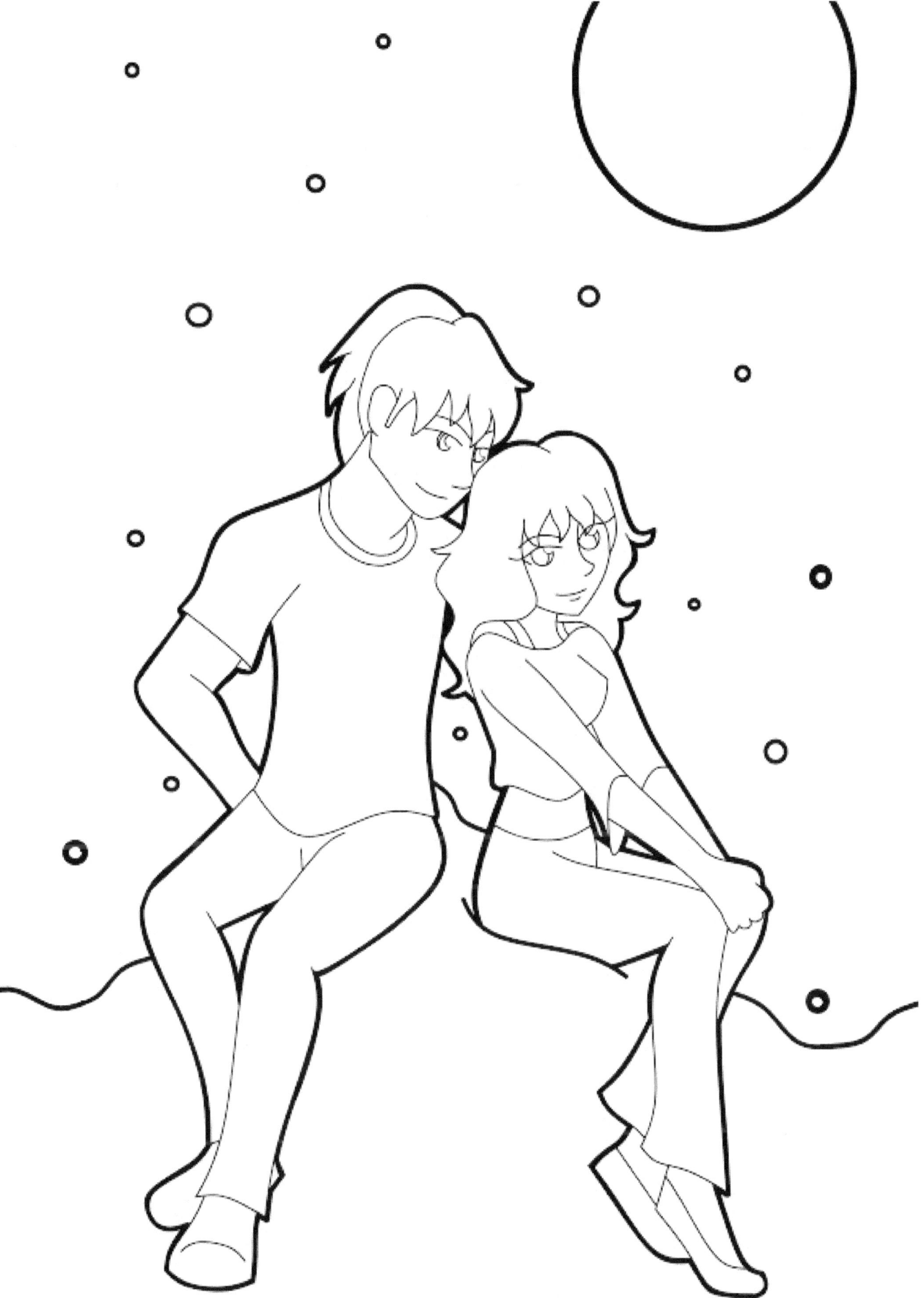

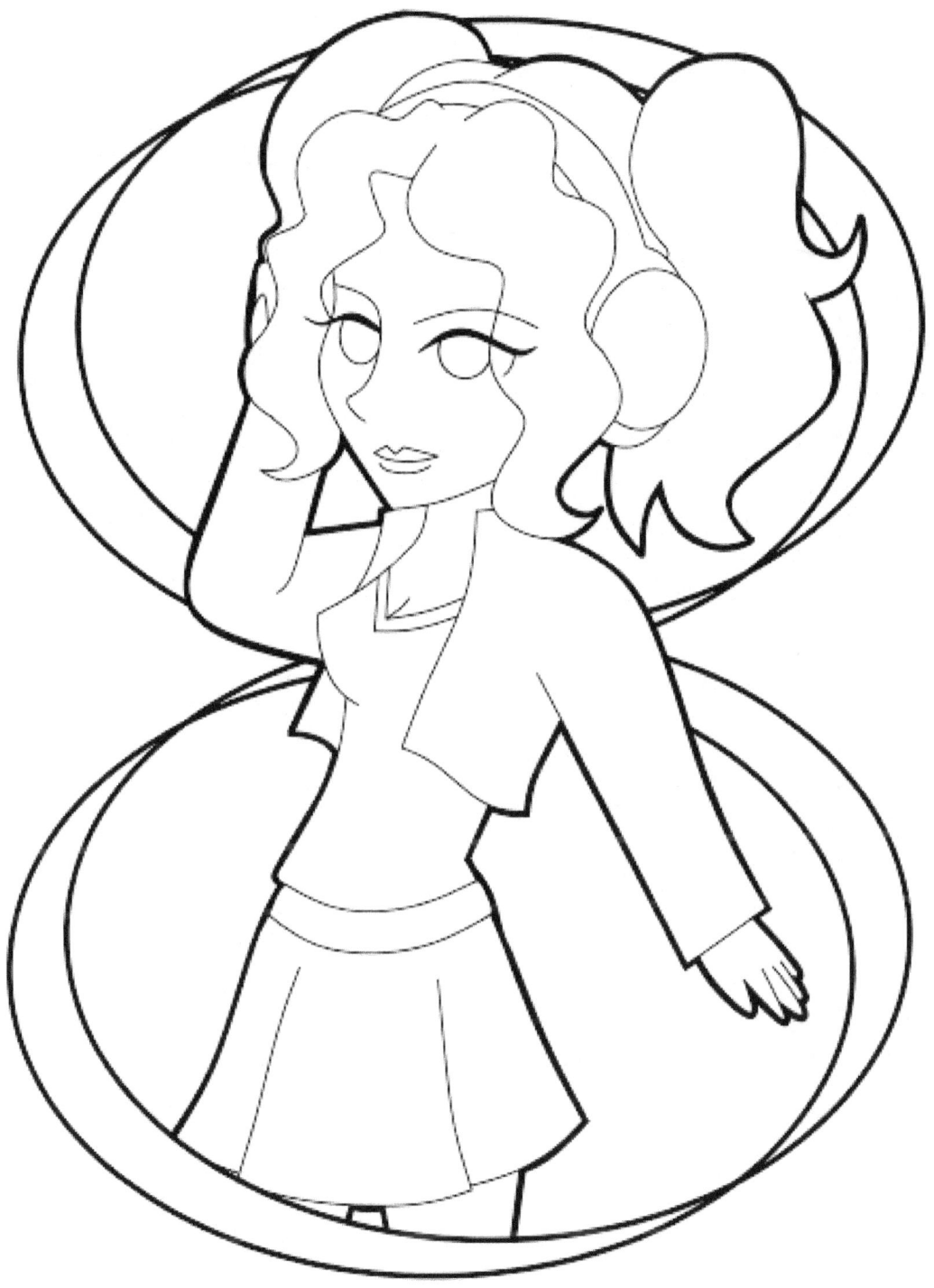

ASHLYNN

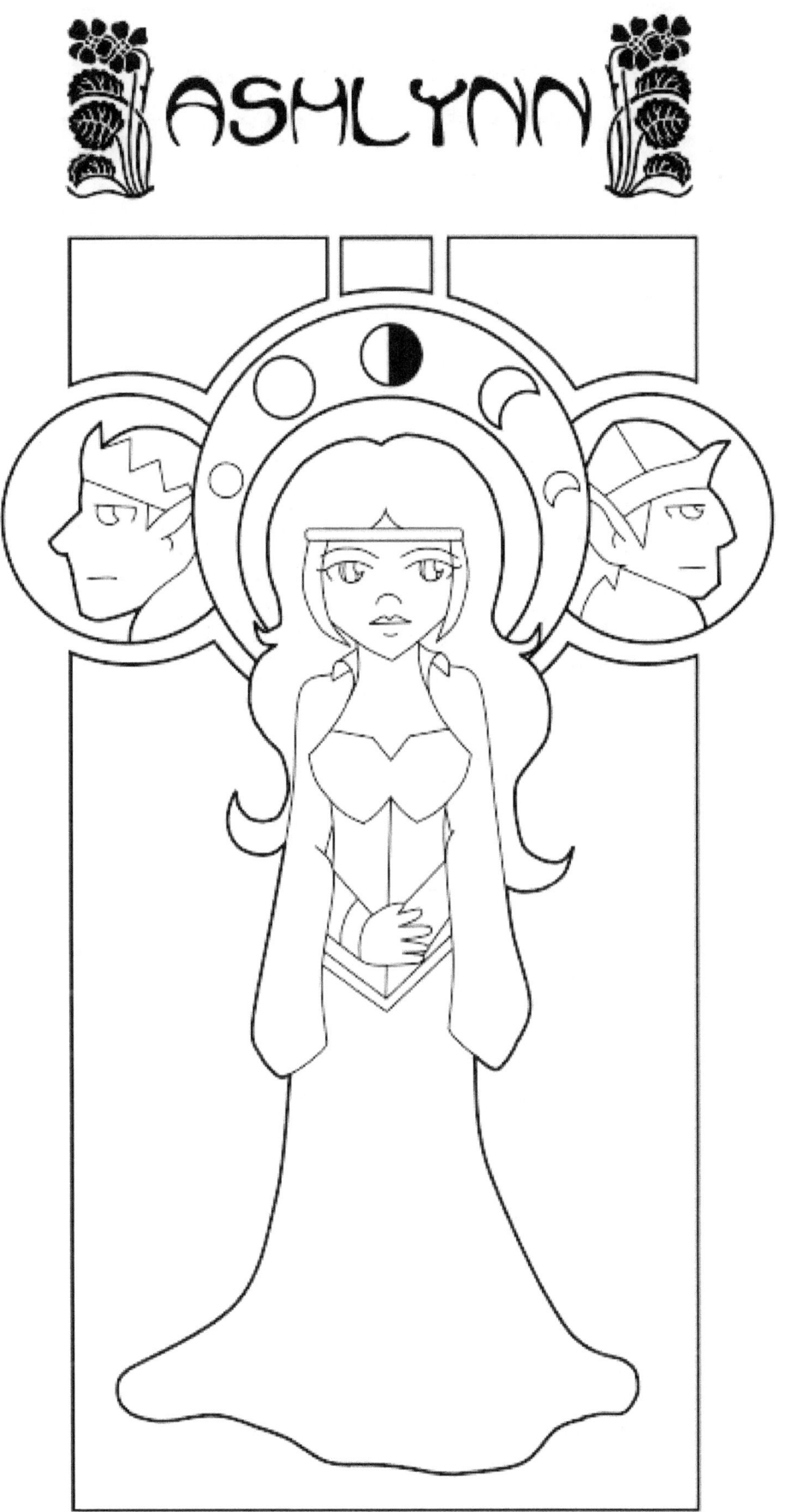

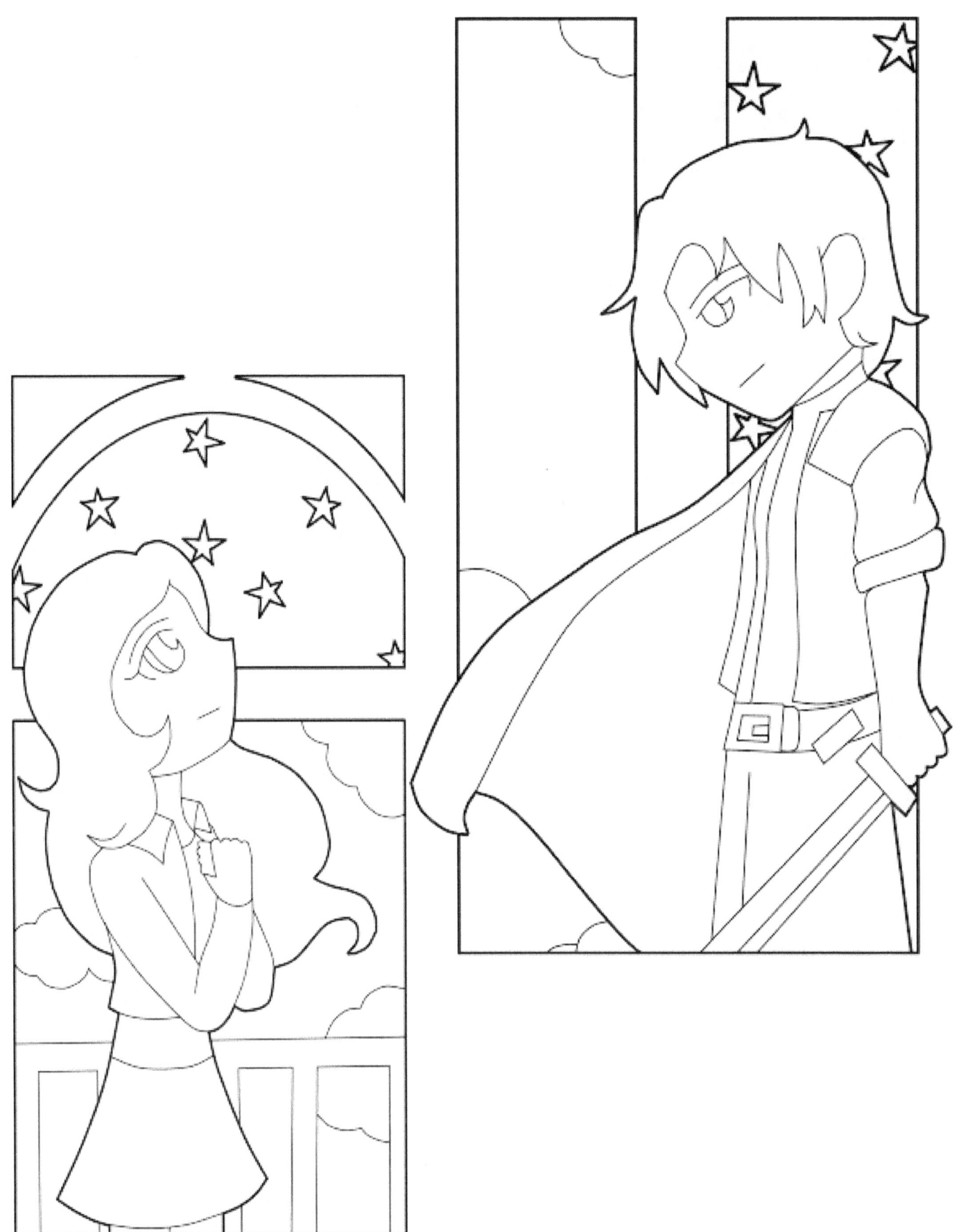

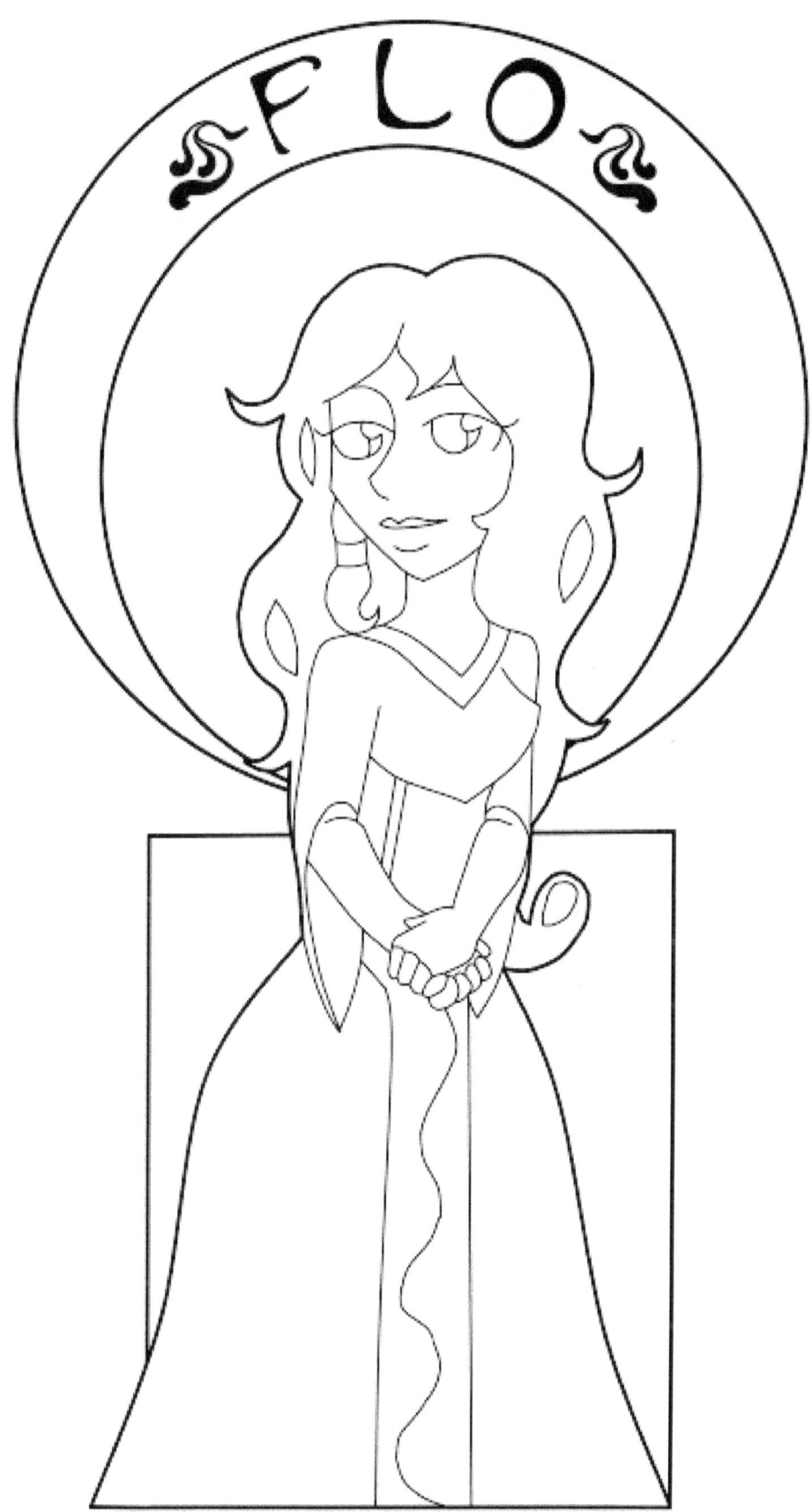

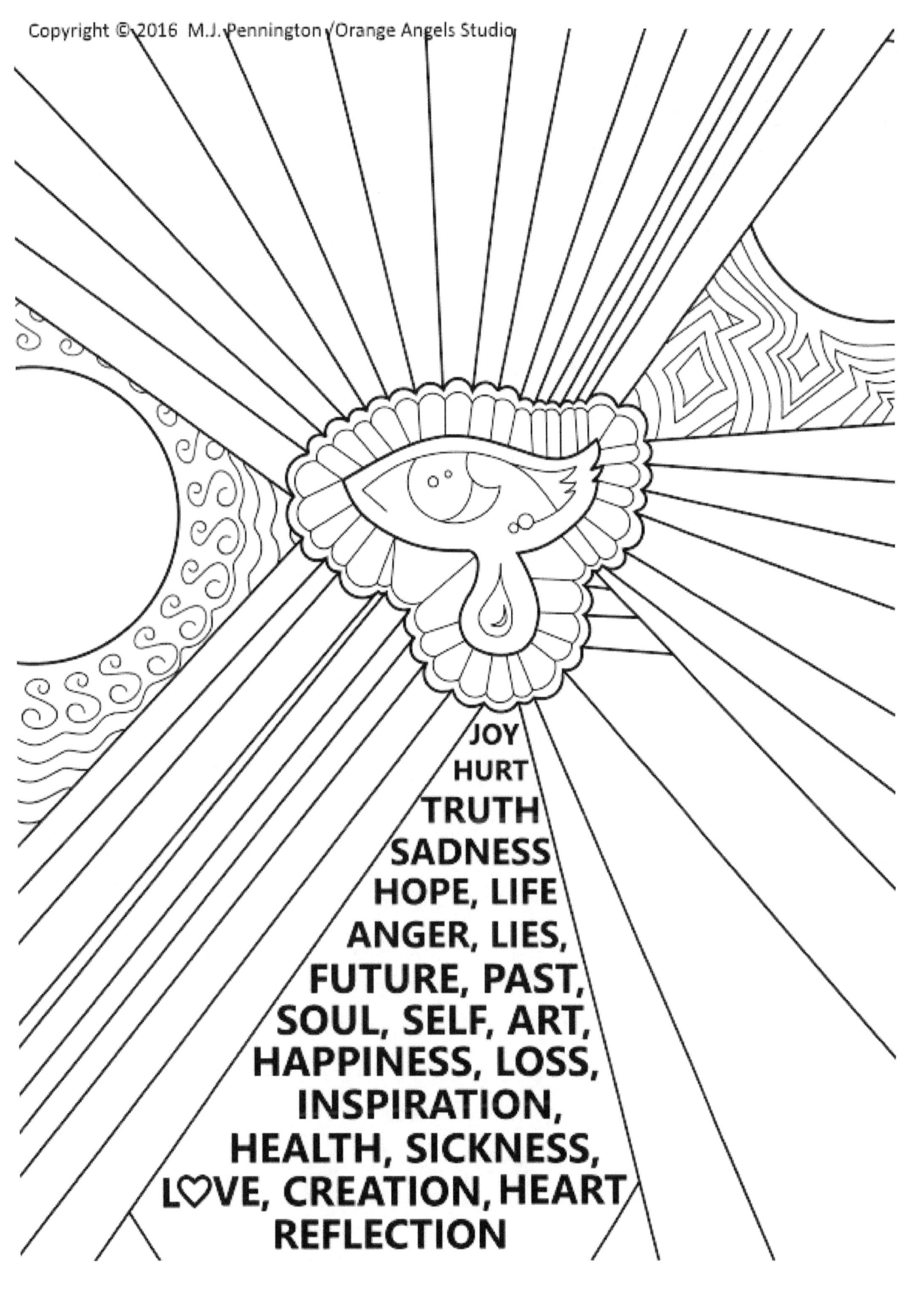

JOY
HURT
TRUTH
SADNESS
HOPE, LIFE
ANGER, LIES,
FUTURE, PAST,
SOUL, SELF, ART,
HAPPINESS, LOSS,
INSPIRATION,
HEALTH, SICKNESS,
LOVE, CREATION, HEART
REFLECTION

About the Artist

M.J. Pennington

M.J. is a mom, Artist, Photographer, and Cosplayer.

If you enjoyed this coloring book please feel free to check out her pictures and other artwork on her studio page:

Orange Angels Studio

www.facebook.com/OrangeAngelsStudio

Like the page for updates on new coloring books, and projects from Orange Angels Studio.

www.ingramcontent.com/pod-product-compliance
Lightning Source LLC
Chambersburg PA
CBHW080721190526
45169CB00006B/2458